For Engineers & Designers

MOI-3D Exercises

200 3D PRACTICE DRAWINGS

SACHIDANAND JHA

Dear Reader,

Thank you for choosing **MOI-3D Exercises** book. This book is part of a family of premium-quality CADIN360 books, all of which are written by Outstanding author who combine practical experience with a gift for teaching.

CADIN360 was founded in 2016. More than 3 years later, we're still committed to producing consistently exceptional books. With each of our titles, we're working hard to set a new standard for the industry. From the paper we print on, to the authors we work with, our goal is to bring you the best books available.

I hope you see all that reflected in these pages. I'd be very interested to hear your comments and get your feedback on how we're doing. Feel free to let me know what you think about this or any other CADIN360 book by sending me an email at contactus@cadin360.com.

If you think you've found a technical error in this book, please visit https://cadin360.com/contact-us/.
Customer feedback is critical to our efforts at CADIN360.

Best regards,

Sachidanand Jha
Founder & CEO, CADIN360

MOI-3D Exercises

Published by
CADIN360
cadin360.com
Copyright © 2019 by CADIN360, All rights reserved.

Limit of Liability/Disclaimer of Warranty:

Examination Copies

Electronic Files

Disclaimer:

Preface

MOI-3D Exercises

❖ This book contain 200 CAD practice exercises and drawings.

❖ This book does not provide step by step tutorial to design 3D models.

❖ S.I Unit is used.

❖ Predominantly used Third Angle Projection.

❖ This book is for **MOI**(Moment of Inspiration) and Other Feature-Based Modeling Software such as Inventor, SolidWorks, NX, Solid Edge, AutoCAD, PTC Creo etc.

❖ It is intended to provide Drafters, Designers and Engineers with enough 3D CAD exercises for practice on **MOI**.

❖ It includes almost all types of exercises that are necessary to provide, clear, concise and systematic information required on industrial machine part drawings.

❖ Third Angle Projection is intentionally used to familiarize Drafters, Designers and Engineers in Third Angle Projection to meet the expectation of world wide Engineering drawing print.

❖ Clear and well drafted drawing help easy understanding of the design.

❖ This book is for Beginner, Intermediate and Advance CAD users.

❖ These exercises are from Basics to Advance level.

❖ Each exercises can be assigned and designed separately.

❖ No Exercise is a prerequisite for another. All dimensions are in mm.

❖ Note: Assume any missing dimensions.

EX-01

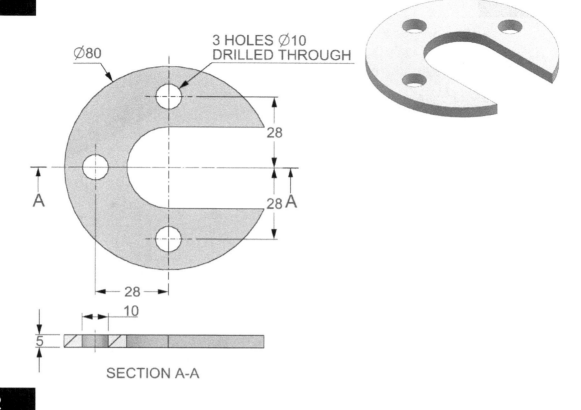

Ø80

3 HOLES Ø10
DRILLED THROUGH

28

28 A

A

28

10

5

SECTION A-A

EX-02

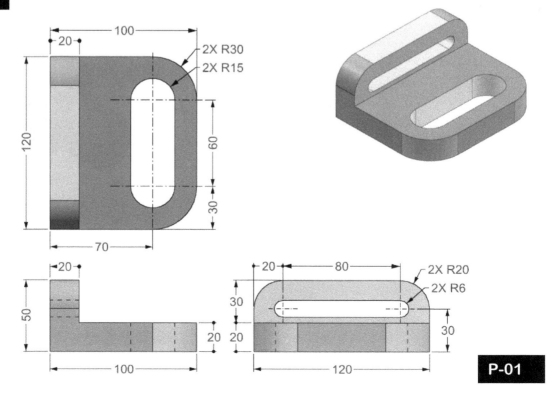

100

20

2X R30

2X R15

120

60

30

70

20

50

100

20

20

30

20

20

80

2X R20

2X R6

30

120

P-01

EX-03

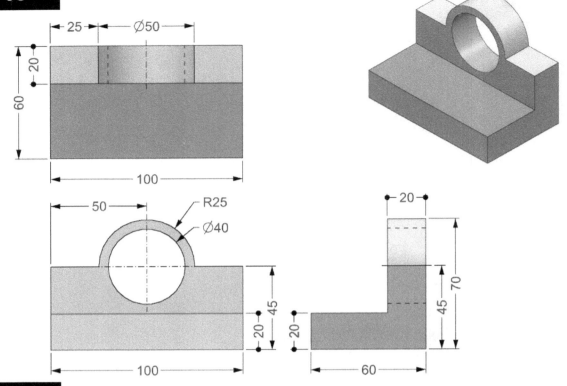

25 | Ø50
20
60
100

50 | R25 | Ø40
45
20 | 20
100

20
70
45
60

EX-04

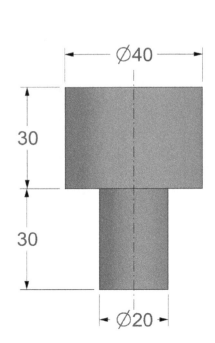

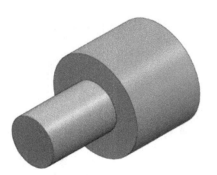

Ø40
30
30
Ø20

P-02

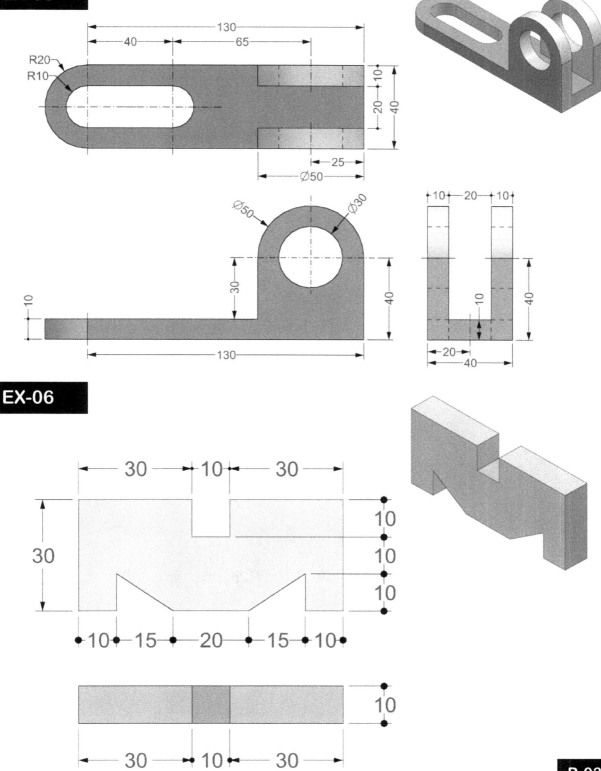

EX-05

EX-06

P-03

EX-07

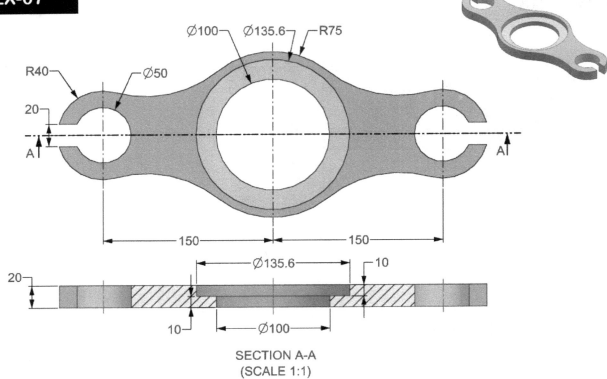

Ø100   Ø135.6   R75
R40   Ø50
20
A
150   150

Ø135.6   10
20
10   Ø100

SECTION A-A
(SCALE 1:1)

EX-08

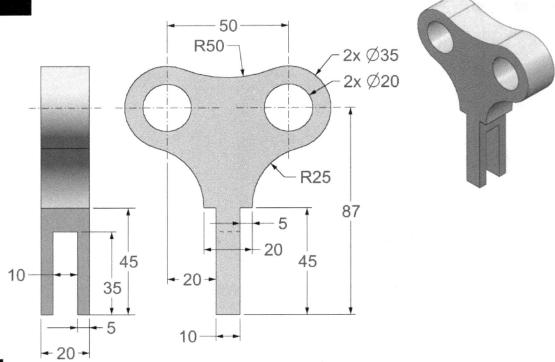

50
R50
2x Ø35
2x Ø20

R25

87

5
20
45

10
45
35
20
20
5
10
20

EX-09

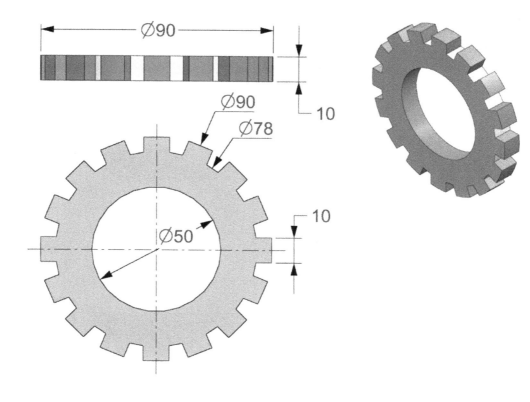

Ø90

Ø90
Ø78
10
Ø50
10

EX-10

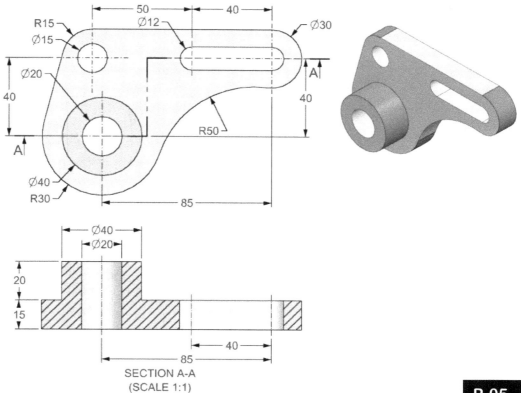

R15
Ø15
Ø12
Ø30
50
40
Ø20
40
40
A
R50
A
85
Ø40
R30

Ø40
Ø20
20
15
40
85

SECTION A-A
(SCALE 1:1)

EX-11

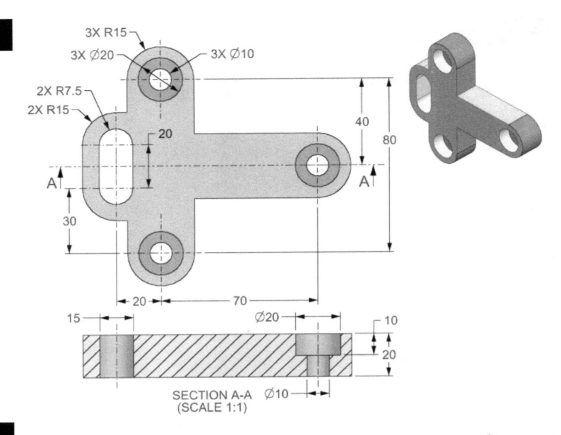

3X R15
3X Ø20
3X Ø10
2X R7.5
2X R15
20
40
80
30
20
70
Ø20

15
10
20
SECTION A-A
(SCALE 1:1)
Ø10

EX-12

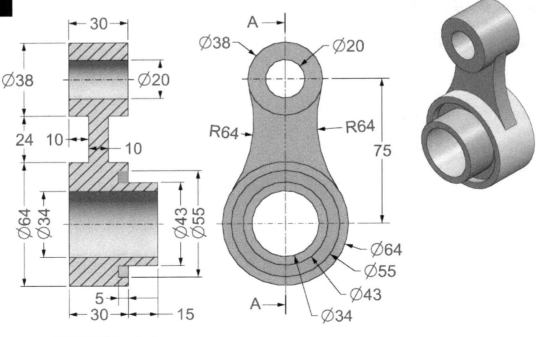

30
Ø38
Ø20
24 10
10
Ø64
Ø34
Ø43
Ø55
5
30
15

A
Ø38
Ø20
R64
R64
75
Ø64
Ø55
Ø43
Ø34
A

SECTION A-A
(SCALE 1:1)

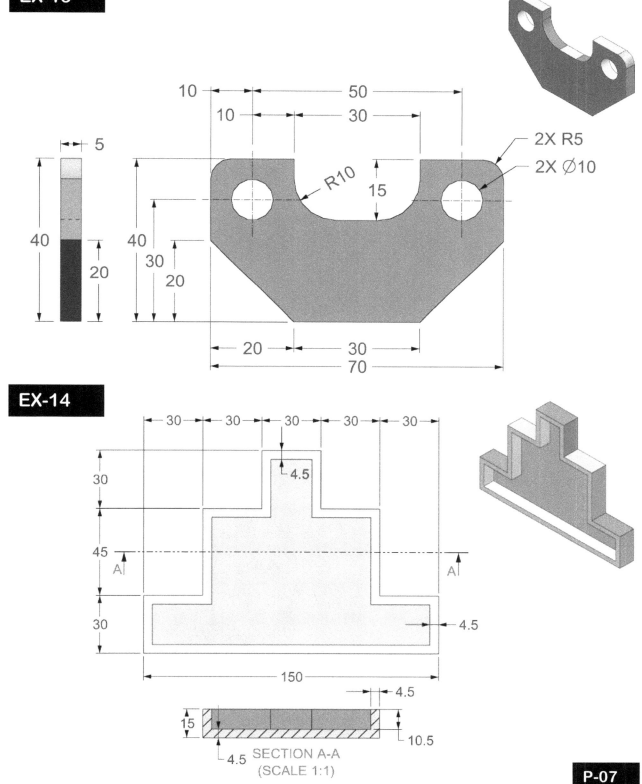

EX-13

10 50
10 30
5
R10
15
2X R5
2X Ø10
40
40 20
30
20
20 30
70

EX-14

30 30 30 30 30
30
4.5
45
A A
30
4.5
150
4.5
15
10.5
4.5 SECTION A-A
(SCALE 1:1)

P-07

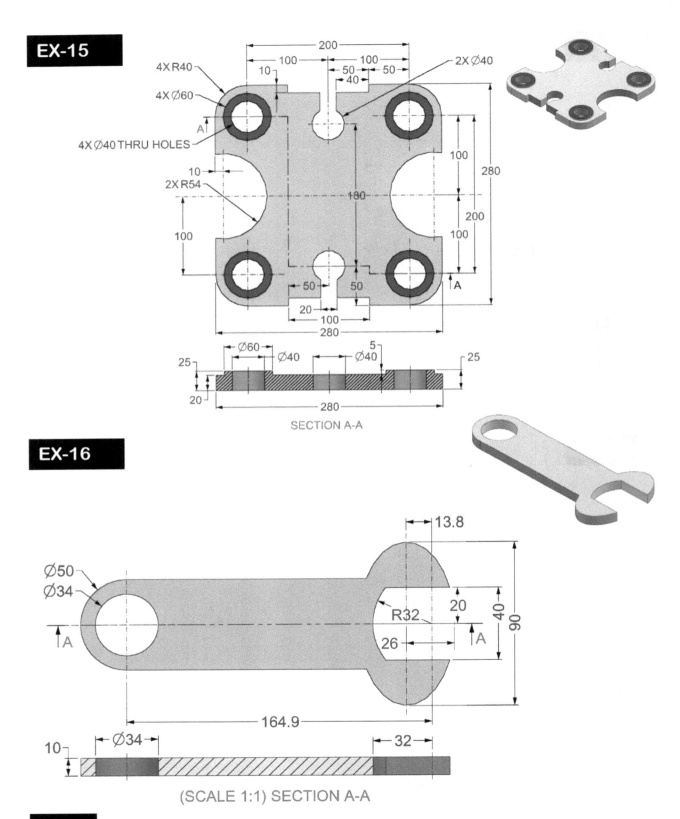

EX-15

4X R40
4X Ø60
4X Ø40 THRU HOLES
2X Ø40
200
100
100
10
50
50
40
A
10
2X R54
100
280
100
180
200
100
100
50
50
20
100
280

SECTION A-A

Ø60
Ø40
Ø40
5
25
25
25
20
280

EX-16

Ø50
Ø34
13.8
R32
20
40
90
26
A
A
164.9

10
Ø34
32

(SCALE 1:1) SECTION A-A

P-08

EX-17

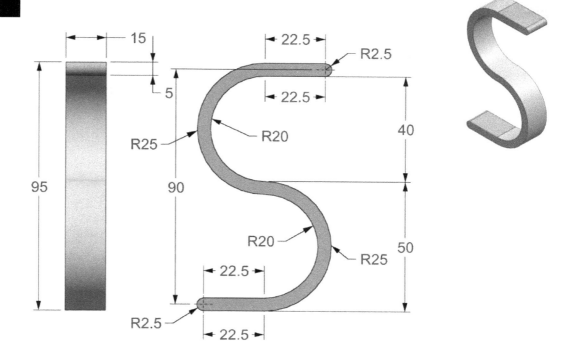

15
5
95
90
22.5
22.5
R2.5
R20
R25
40
50
R20
R25
22.5
R2.5
22.5

EX-18

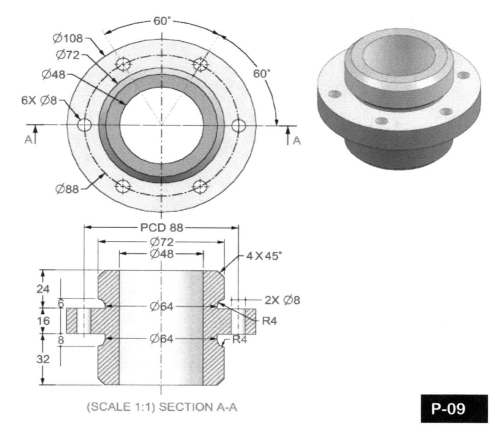

60°
Ø108
Ø72
Ø48
6X Ø8
60°
A
A
Ø88

PCD 88
Ø72
Ø48
4 X 45°
24
6
Ø64
2X Ø8
R4
16
8
Ø64
R4
32

(SCALE 1:1) SECTION A-A

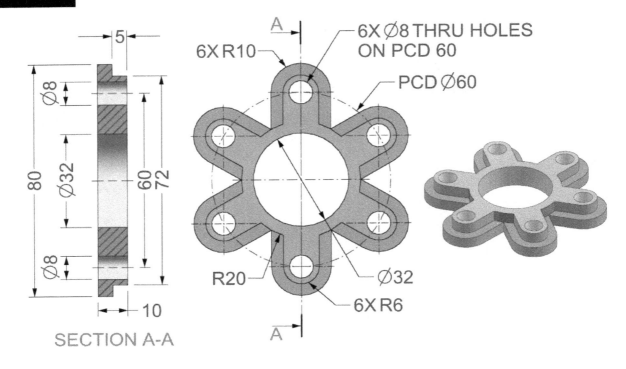

6X R10

6X Ø8 THRU HOLES
ON PCD 60

PCD Ø60

5

Ø8

Ø32

80

60

72

Ø8

10

R20

Ø32

6X R6

A

A

SECTION A-A

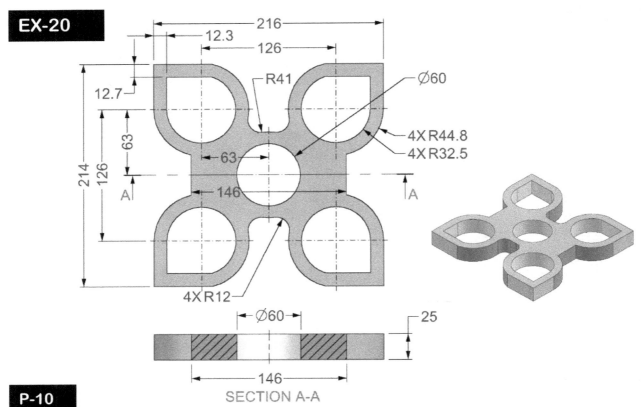

216

12.3

126

12.7

R41

Ø60

63

63

4X R44.8
4X R32.5

214

126

A

146

A

4X R12

Ø60

25

146

SECTION A-A

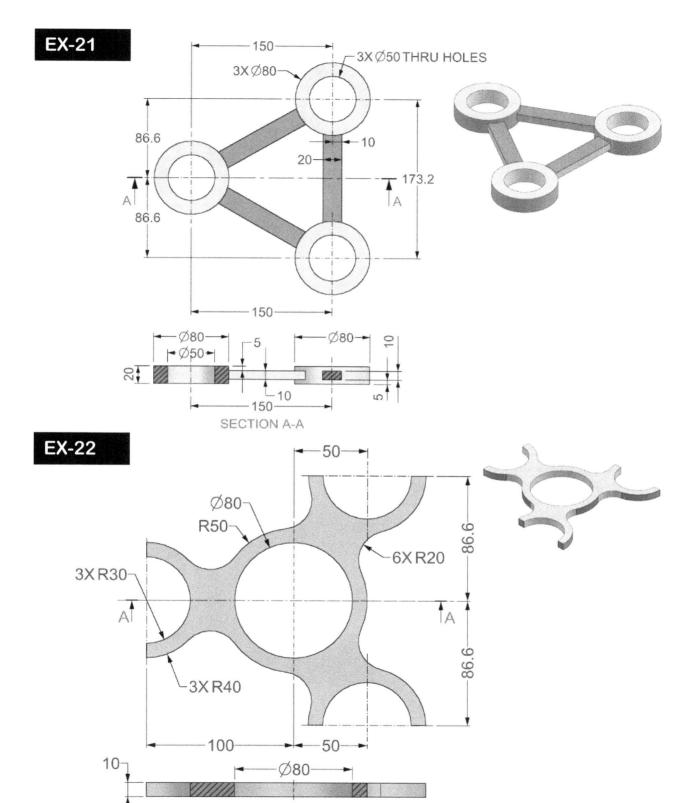

EX-21

150
3X Ø50 THRU HOLES
3X Ø80
86.6
10
20
173.2
86.6
A
A
150

Ø80
Ø50
5
Ø80
10
20
10
5
150

SECTION A-A

EX-22

50
Ø80
R50
86.6
6X R20
3X R30
A
A
3X R40
86.6
100
50

10
Ø80

SECTION A-A

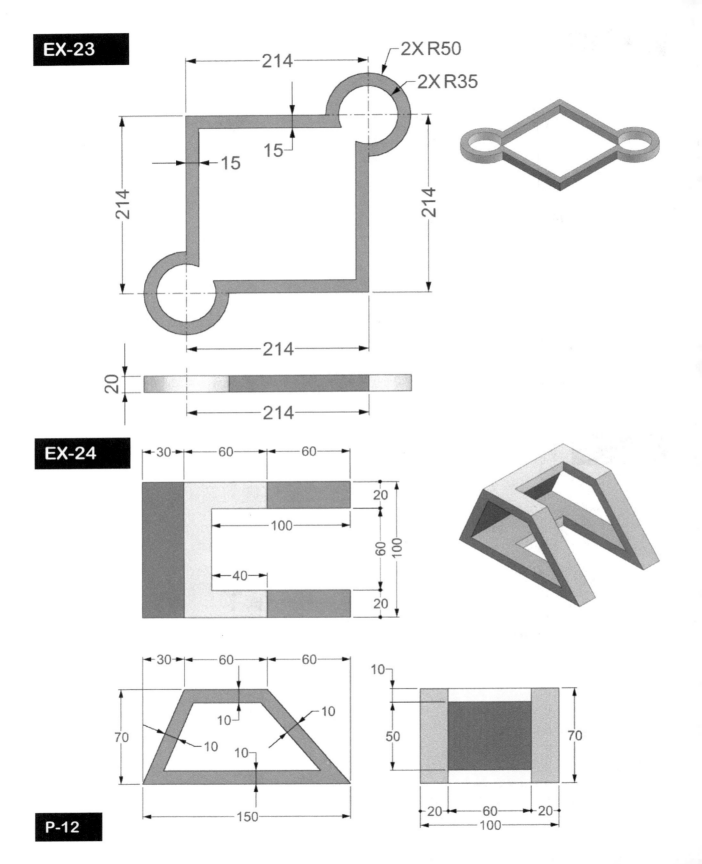

EX-23

2X R50
2X R35
214
214
214
214
15
15
20
214

EX-24

30
60
60
20
100
60
100
40
20

P-12

30
60
60
10
10
10
10
70
150

10
50
70
20
60
20
100

EX-25

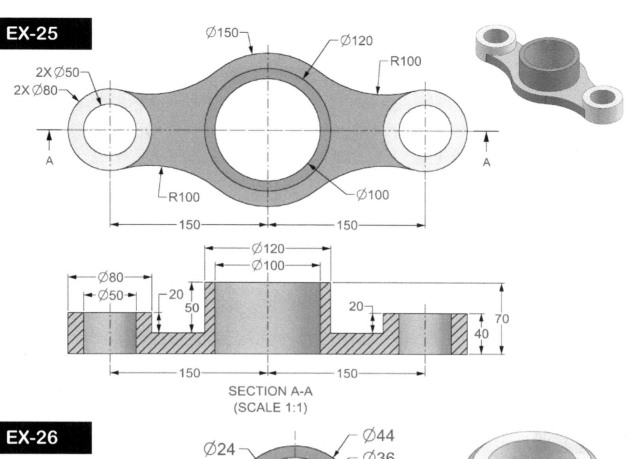

Ø150
Ø120
R100
2X Ø50
2X Ø80
R100
Ø100
150
150
A
A

Ø120
Ø100
Ø80
Ø50
20
50
20
70
40
150
150

SECTION A-A
(SCALE 1:1)

EX-26

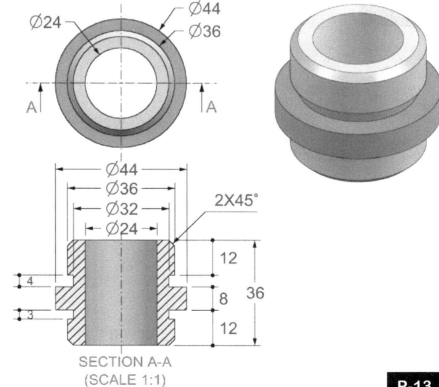

Ø24
Ø44
Ø36

A
A

Ø44
Ø36
Ø32
Ø24
2X45°
12
4
8
36
3
12

SECTION A-A
(SCALE 1:1)

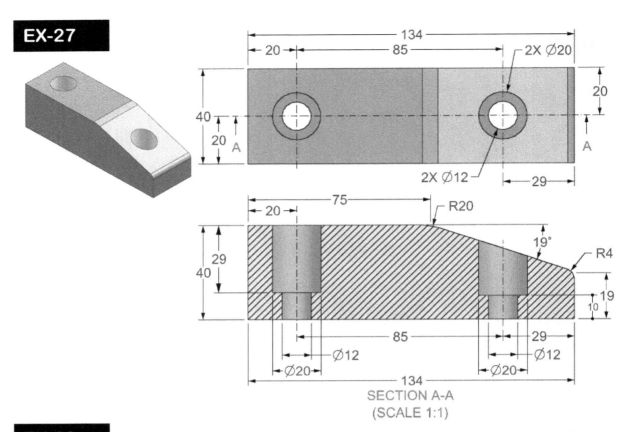

134
20
85
2X ⌀20
40
20
20
A
A
2X ⌀12
29

20
75
R20
29
19°
R4
40
19
10
85
29
⌀12
⌀12
⌀20
⌀20
134

SECTION A-A
(SCALE 1:1)

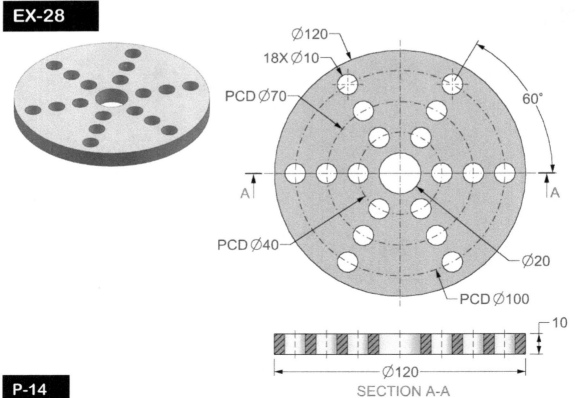

⌀120
18X ⌀10
PCD ⌀70
60°
PCD ⌀40
⌀20
PCD ⌀100
10
⌀120
SECTION A-A

EX-29

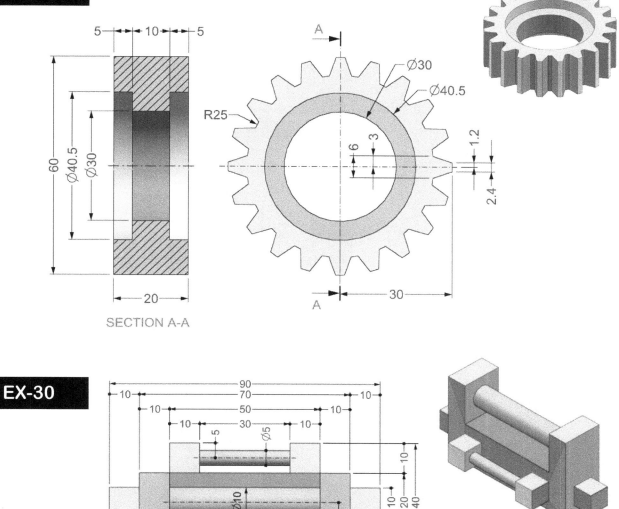

SECTION A-A

EX-30

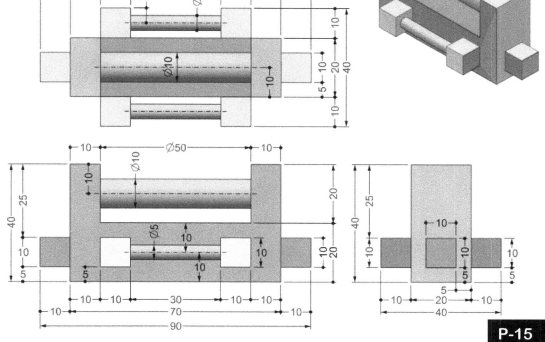

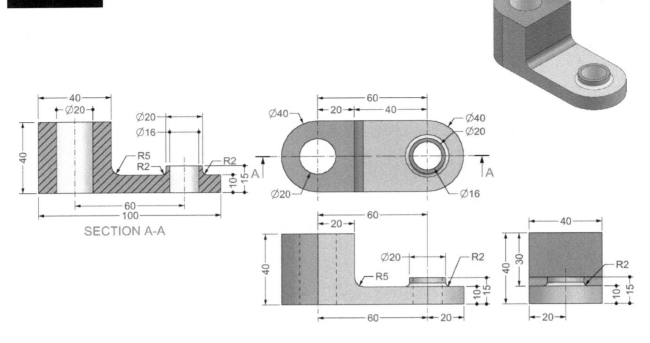

SECTION A-A

EX-32

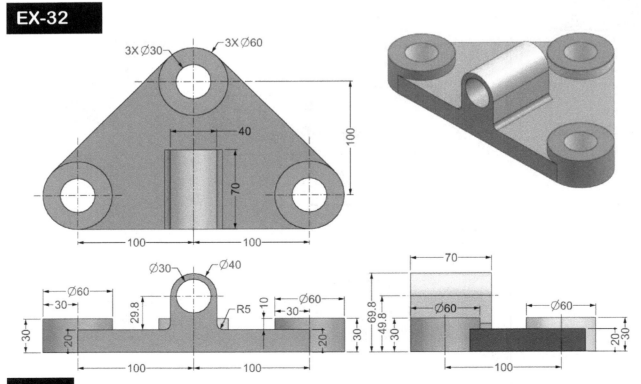

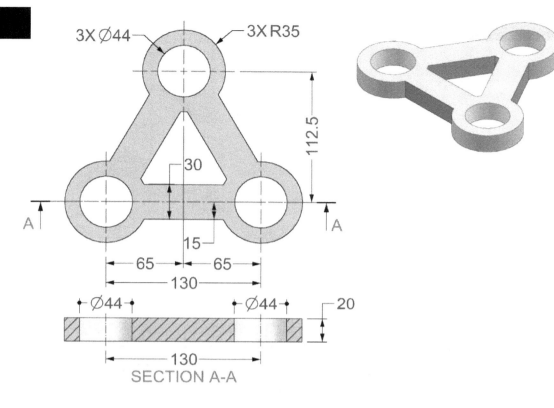

3X Ø44 3X R35

112.5

30

15

65 65

130

Ø44 Ø44 20

130

SECTION A-A

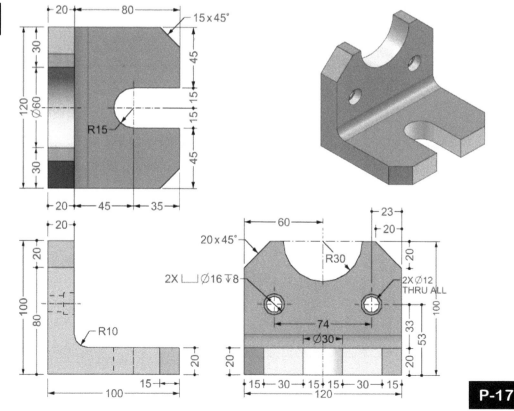

20 80 15 x 45°

30

120 45

Ø60

15 15

R15 15 15

30 45

20 45 35

20

20

100

80

R10

15 20

100

23

60 20

20 x 45° R30

20

2X ⌴Ø16 ⤓8 2X Ø12
THRU ALL

74 100

Ø30 33 53

20 20

15 30 15 15 30 15
120

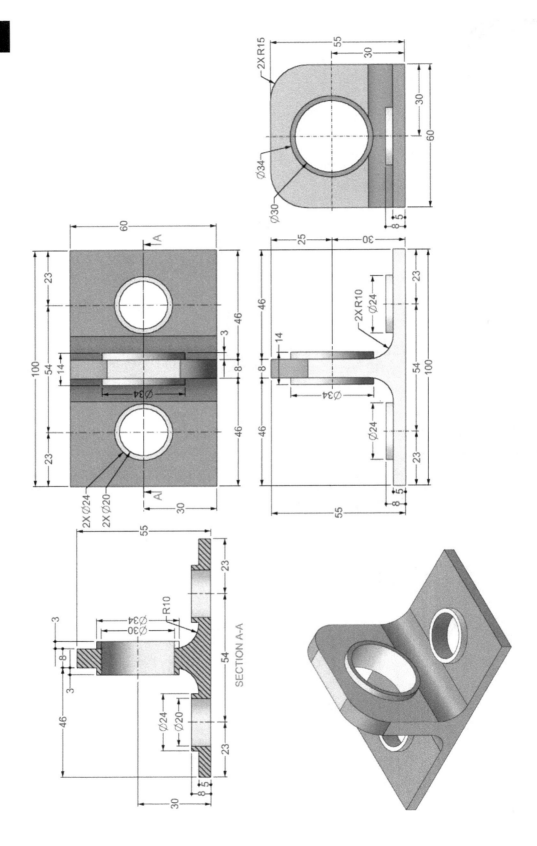

SECTION A-A

EX-36

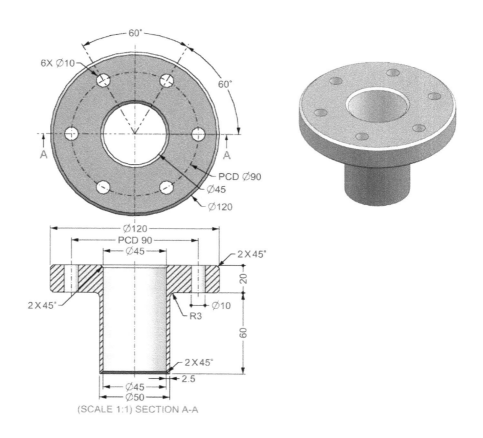

60°

6X Ø10

60°

PCD Ø90

Ø45

Ø120

Ø120

PCD 90

Ø45

2 X 45°

20

2 X 45°

Ø10

R3

60

2 X 45°

2.5

Ø45

Ø50

(SCALE 1:1) SECTION A-A

EX-37

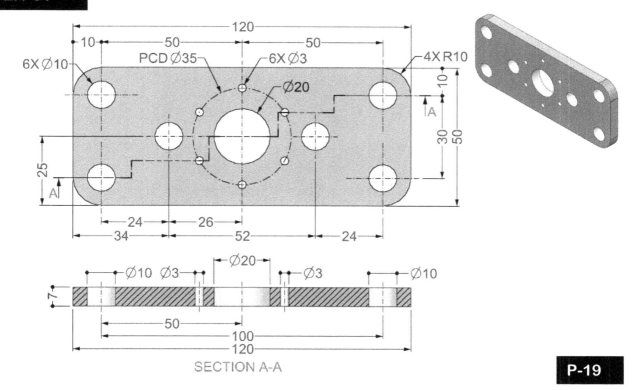

120

10

50

50

6X Ø10

PCD Ø35

6X Ø3

4X R10

Ø20

10

A

30

50

25

A

24

26

52

24

34

Ø10   Ø3

Ø20

Ø3

Ø10

7

50

100

120

SECTION A-A

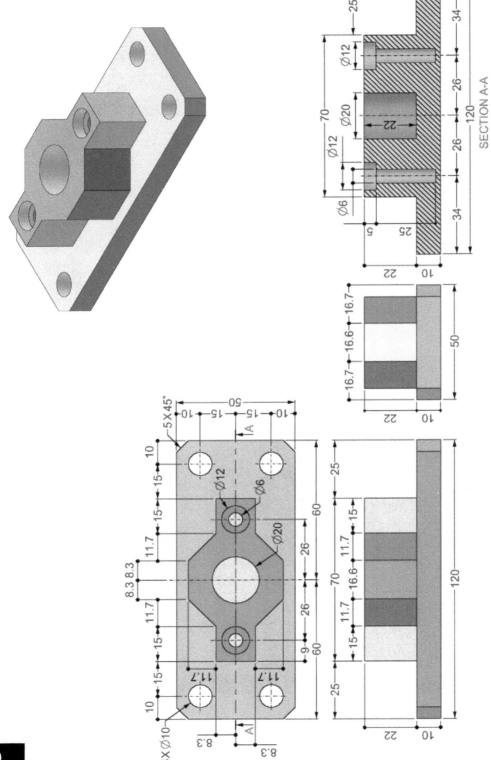

SECTION A-A

EX-39

70
R20
Ø20
40
45

R25
Ø20
45
20
30
10
10
A — A
45
65

20
2X R10
Ø40
Ø20
25
45
SECTION A-A

EX-40

Ø60
20
10
5
Ø50

Ø60
Ø50

5 — 10 — 5
30
Ø60
20

P-21

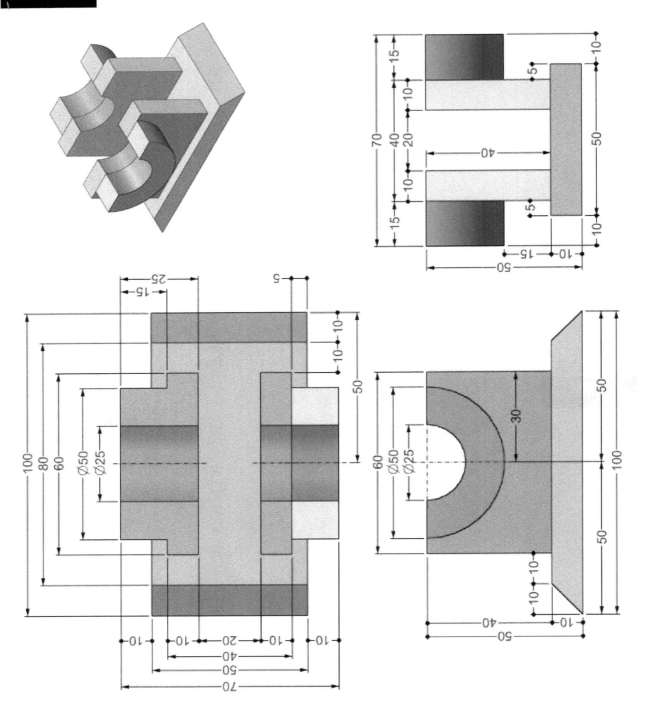

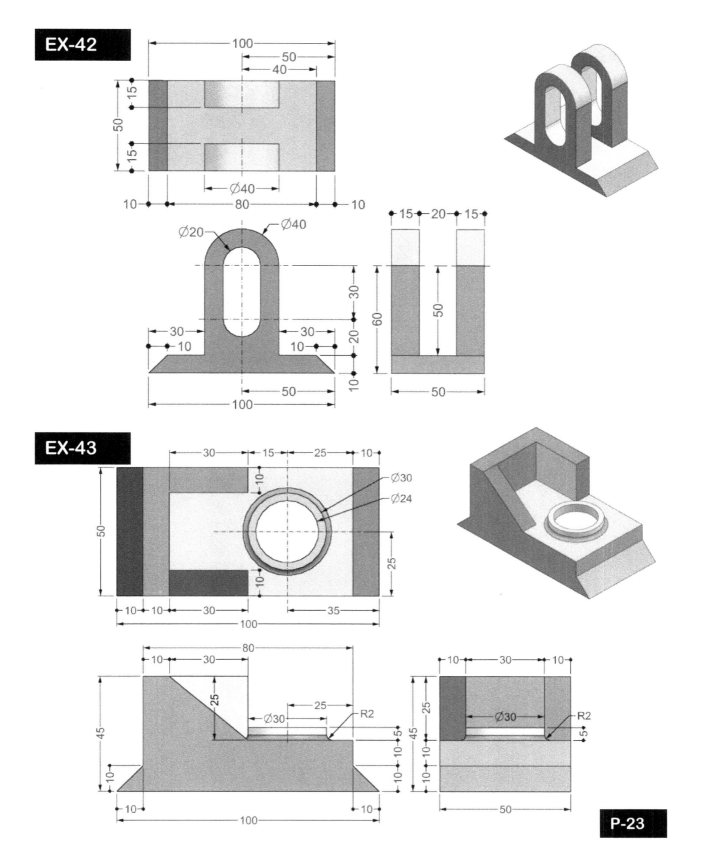

EX-42

EX-43

P-23

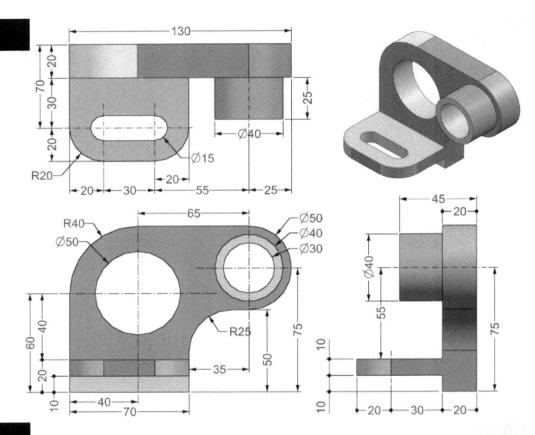

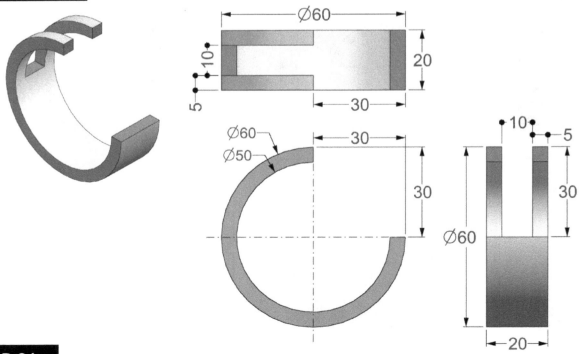

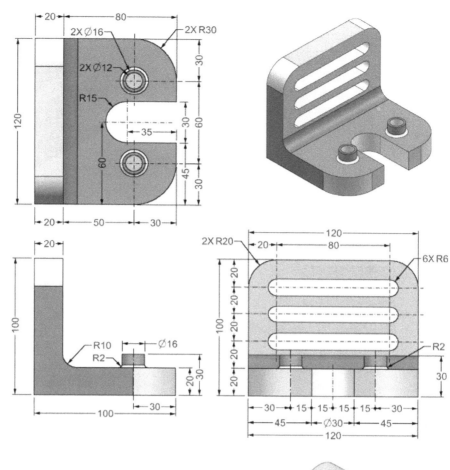

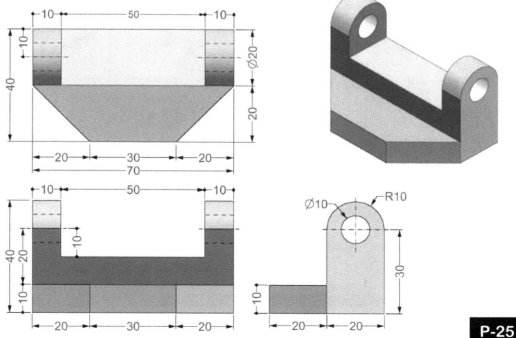

EX-48

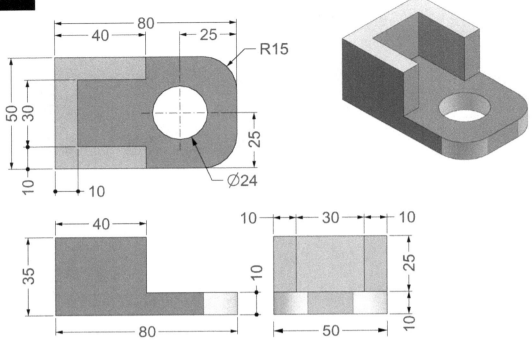

EX-49

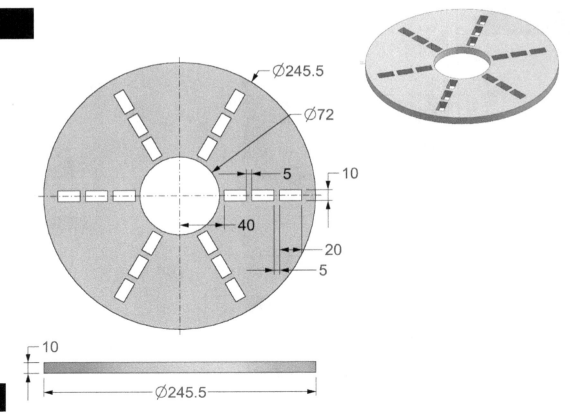

P-26

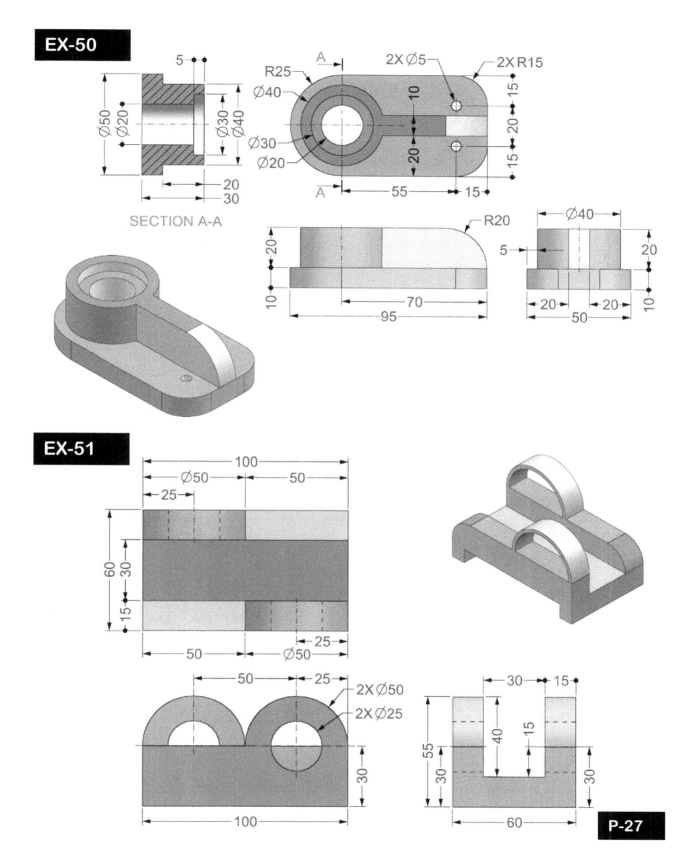

EX-50

5
Ø50
Ø20
Ø30
Ø40
20
30

SECTION A-A

R25
Ø40
Ø30
Ø20
A
2X Ø5
2X R15
10
15
20
15
20
15
55
15

R20
20
10
70
95

Ø40
5
20
20
20
50
10

EX-51

100
Ø50
50
25
60
30
15
50
Ø50
25

50
25
2X Ø50
2X Ø25
30
100

30
15
55
40
15
30
30
60

P-27

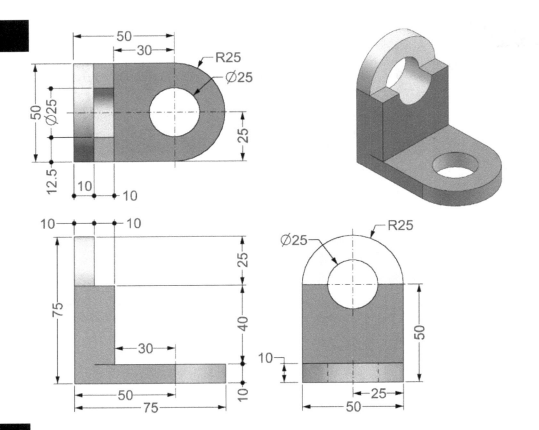

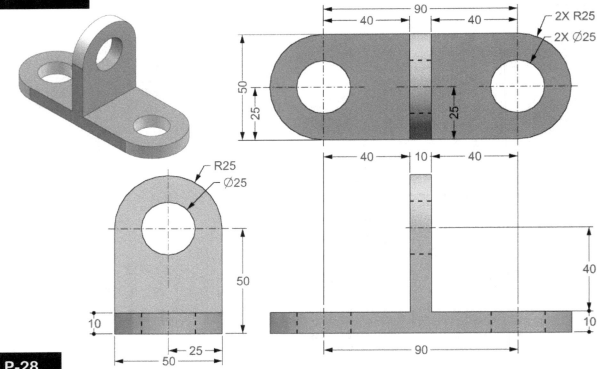

EX-54

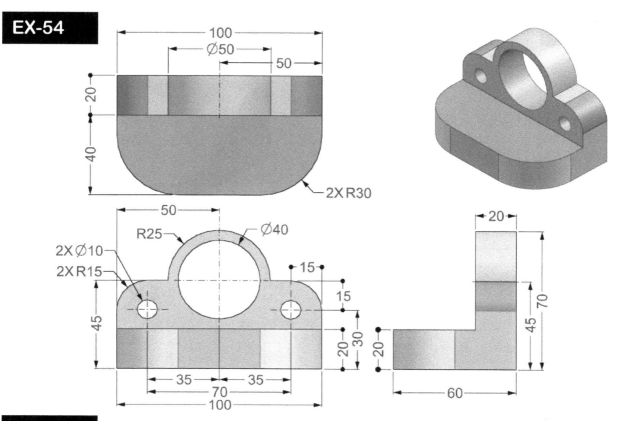

EX-55

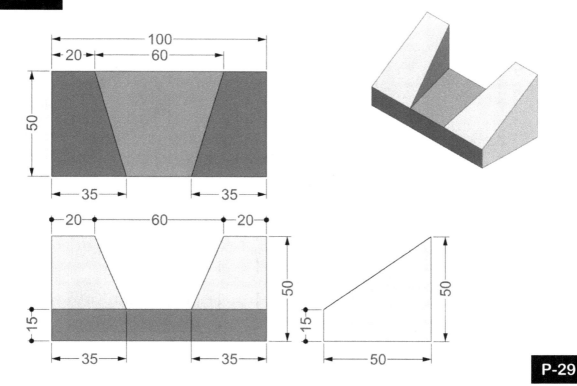

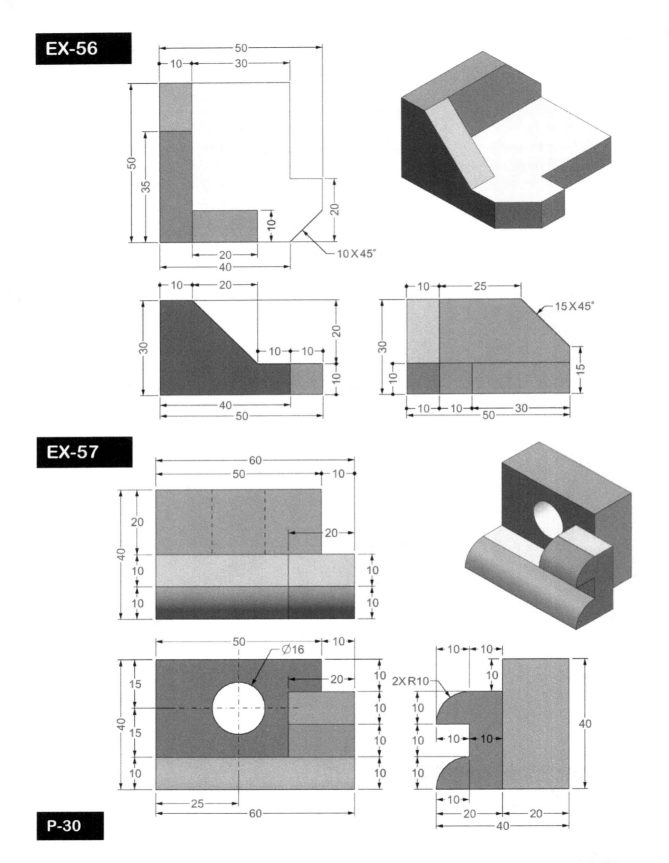

EX-56

EX-57

P-30

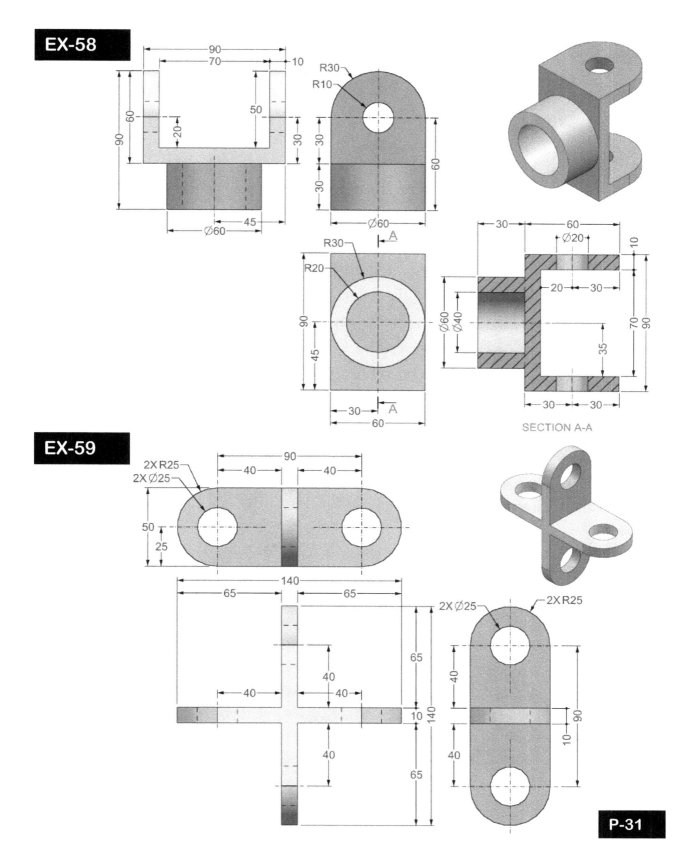

EX-58

90
70
10
R30
R10
60
50
90
20
30
45
Ø60
Ø60
A
R30
R20
90
45
30
A
60

30
60
Ø20
20
30
10
Ø60
Ø40
35
70
90
30
30
SECTION A-A

EX-59

2X R25
2X Ø25
90
40
40
50
25
140
65
65
65
40
40
40
10
40
65
2X Ø25
2X R25
40
90
10
40

P-31

EX-60

Ø50
2X Ø10
22.5
15
25
60
43.9
10
15
25
50
45
95

Ø50
Ø40
R4 R10
R10
10
40
155
130
80
140
10
45 45
R10
R10
55
40
30
10 10
22.5 22.5
100

60
85.4
100
155
34.6
10 25
40
60

EX-61

Ø120
20
R3
50
Ø50
R2
10,10,10
Ø50
Ø70

14 14
PCD Ø90
R60
Ø70
Ø30
Ø50
6X Ø10
66
132
14 14
14
A
A
66
66 66
132

132
Ø70
Ø50
Ø30
Ø10
10 10
10
10
10
Ø50
Ø30
R2
50
100
R3
Ø10
20
45 45
90
Ø120
SECTION A-A

Ø120
6X Ø10
ON PCD 90
PCD Ø90
Ø30
66
132
14 14
14 14
66
66 66
132

P-32

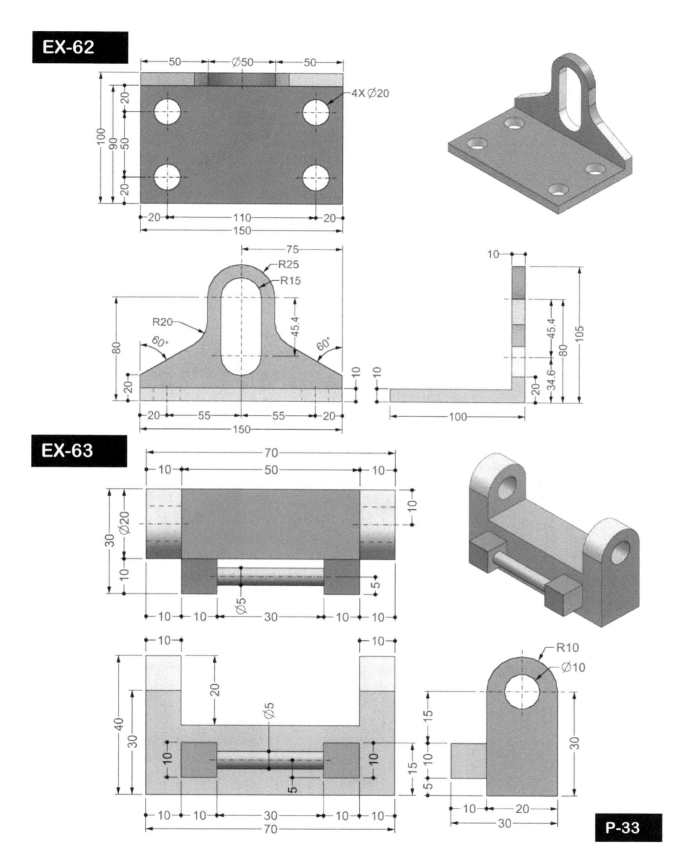

EX-62

EX-63

P-33

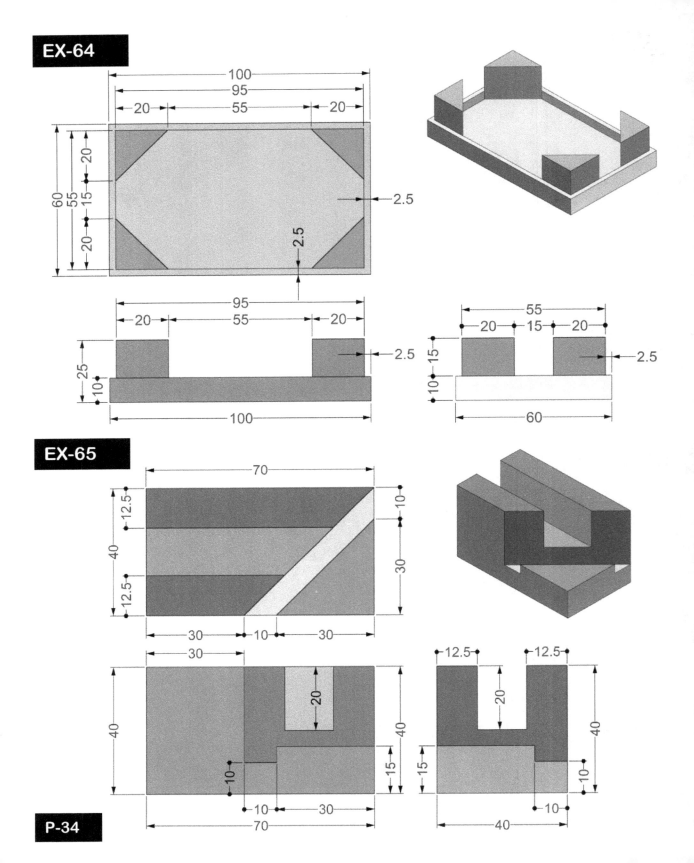

EX-64

EX-65

P-34

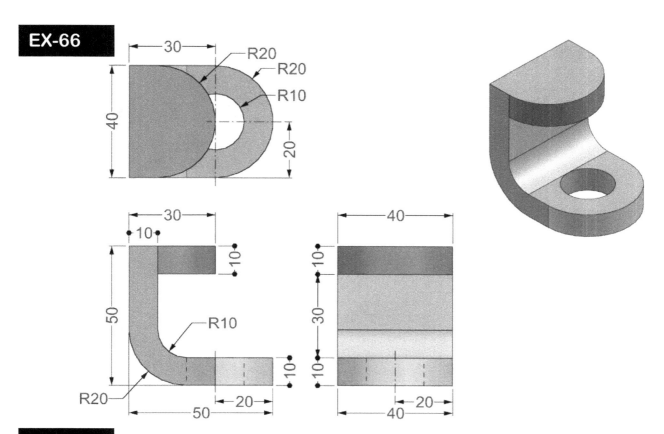

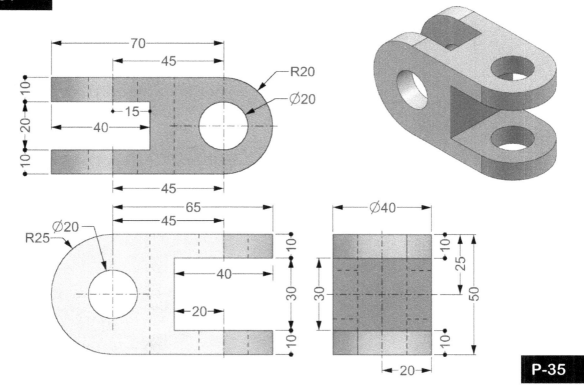

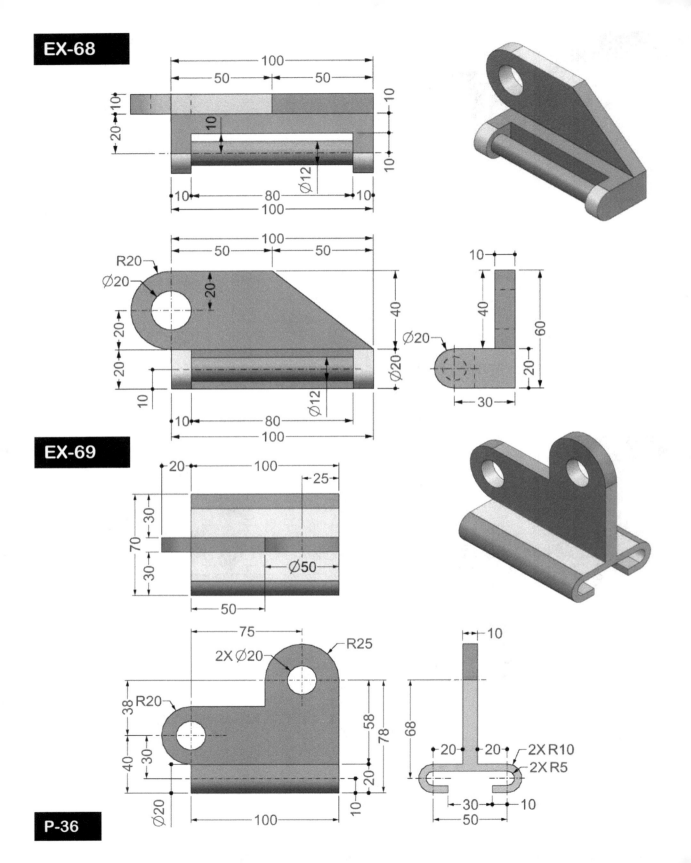

EX-68

EX-69

P-36

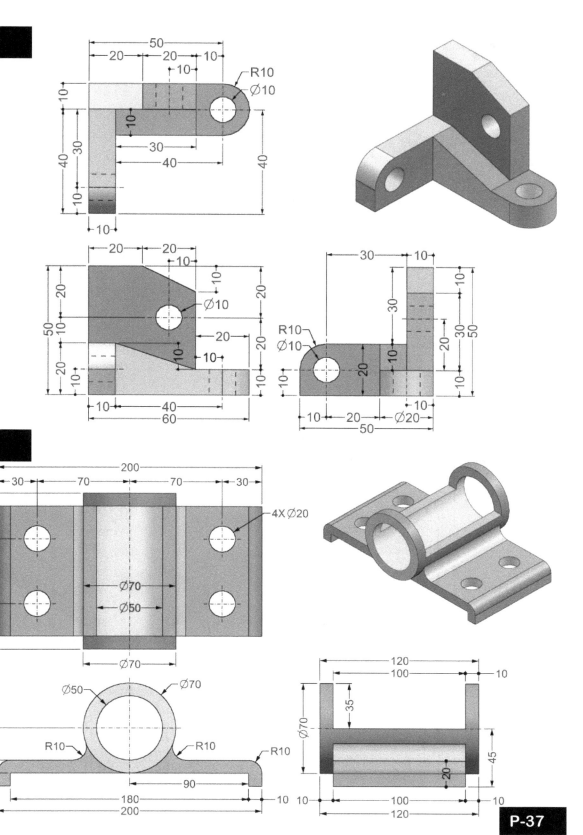

EX-70

EX-71

P-37

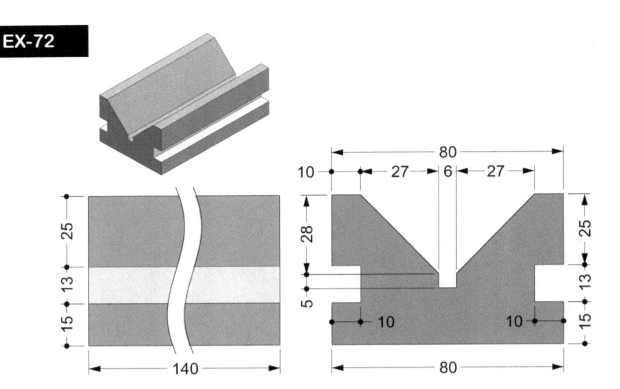

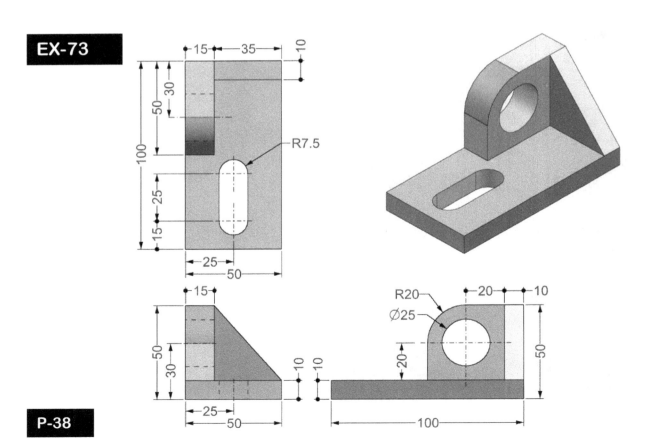

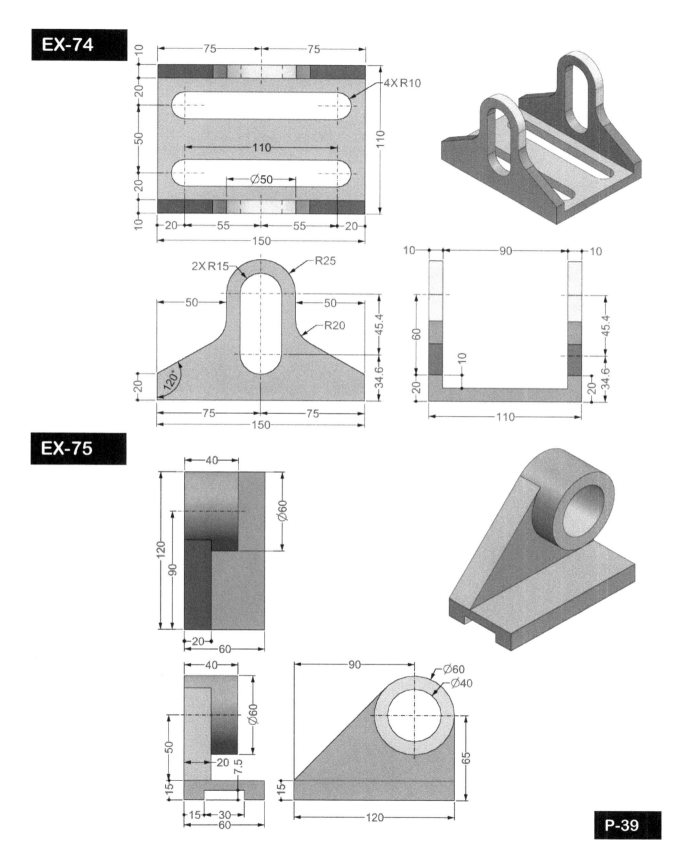

EX-74

EX-75

EX-76

EX-77

SECTION A-A

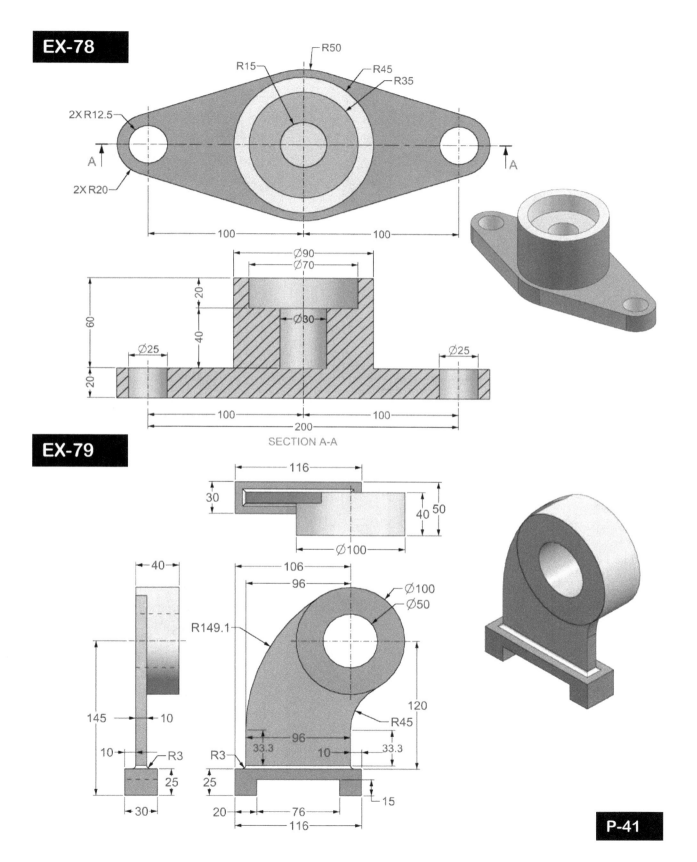

EX-78

R50
R15
R45
R35
2X R12.5
A
A
2X R20
100
100

Ø90
Ø70
20
60
40
Ø30
Ø25
Ø25
20
100
100
200
SECTION A-A

EX-79

116
30
40 50
Ø100

40
106
96
Ø100
Ø50
R149.1
145
10
120
10
R3
R45
96
R3
33.3
10
33.3
25
25
15
30
20
76
116

P-41

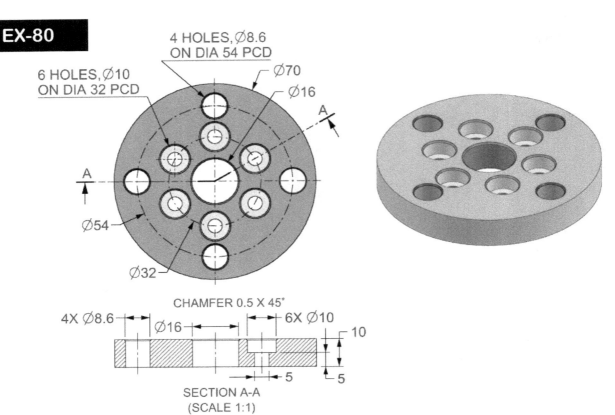

6 HOLES,∅10
ON DIA 32 PCD

4 HOLES,∅8.6
ON DIA 54 PCD

∅70

∅16

A

A

∅54

∅32

CHAMFER 0.5 X 45°

4X ∅8.6

∅16

6X ∅10

10

5

5

SECTION A-A
(SCALE 1:1)

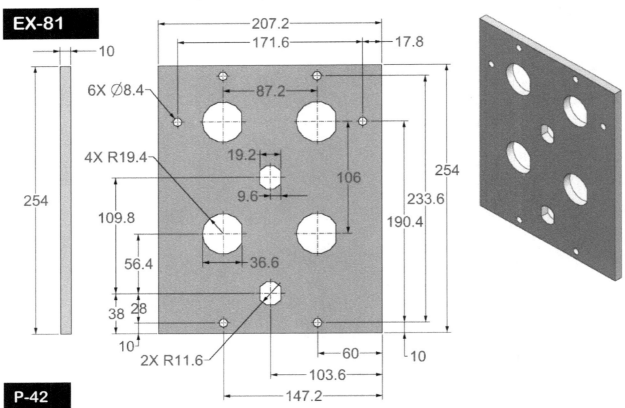

10

207.2

171.6

17.8

6X ∅8.4

87.2

4X R19.4

19.2

9.6

106

254

233.6

190.4

109.8

56.4

36.6

38 28

10

2X R11.6

60

10

103.6

147.2

254

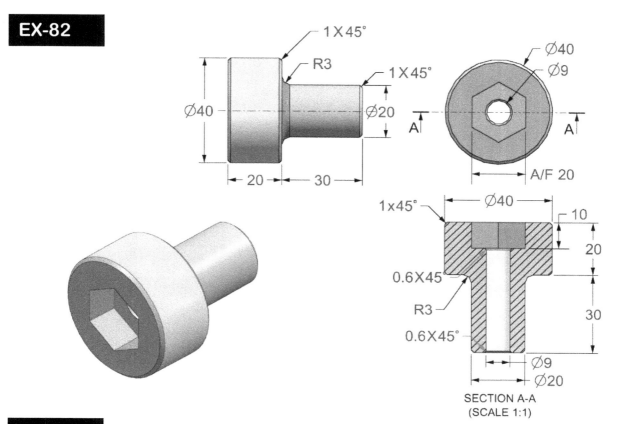

1 X 45°
R3
1 X 45°
Ø40
Ø40
Ø9
Ø20
A
A
20
30
A/F 20

1x45°
Ø40
10
20
0.6X45
R3
0.6X45°
30
Ø9
Ø20

SECTION A-A
(SCALE 1:1)

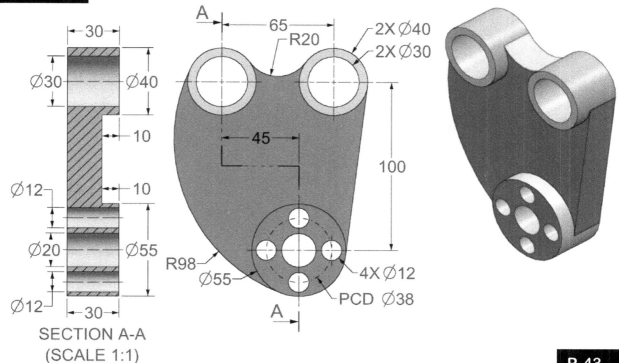

30
Ø30
Ø40
10
10
Ø12
Ø20
Ø55
Ø12
30

SECTION A-A
(SCALE 1:1)

A
65
R20
2X Ø40
2X Ø30
45
100
R98
Ø55
4X Ø12
PCD Ø38
A

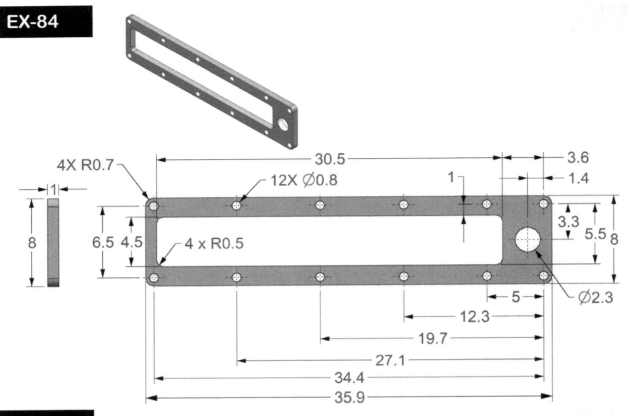

4X R0.7
12X ⌀0.8
4 x R0.5
30.5
3.6
1.4
1
3.3
5.5
8
⌀2.3
5
12.3
19.7
27.1
34.4
35.9
1
8
6.5 4.5

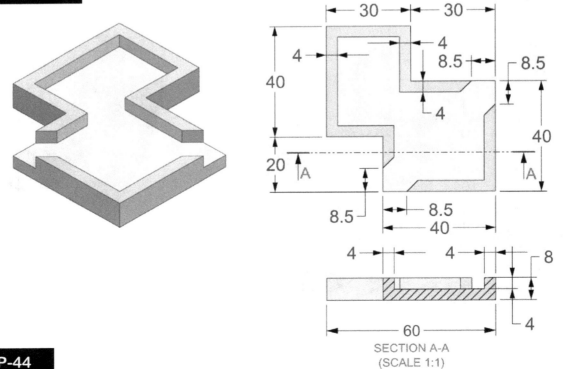

30
30
4
4
8.5
8.5
40
4
40
20
A
A
8.5
8.5
40
4
4
8
60
4

SECTION A-A
(SCALE 1:1)

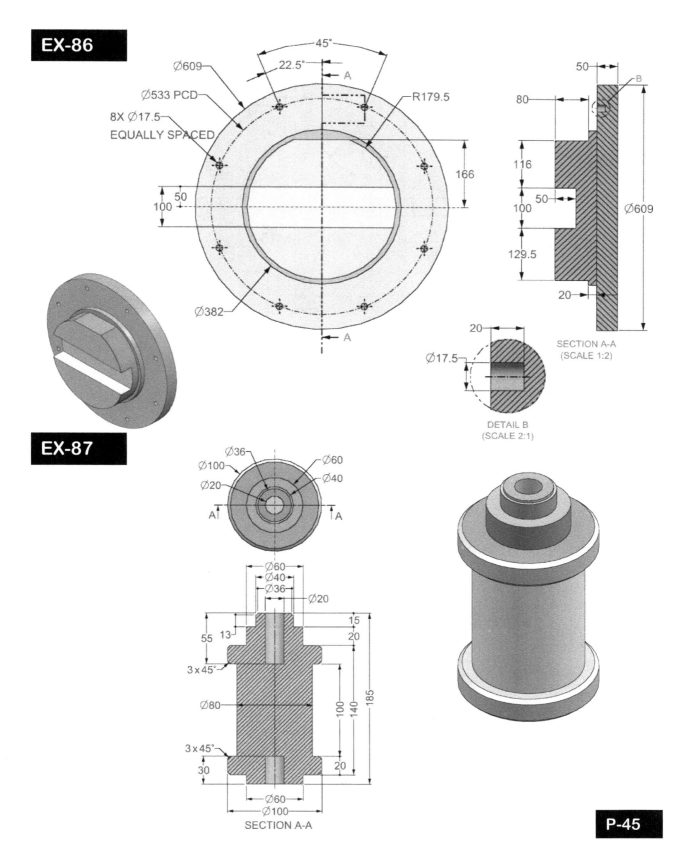

EX-86

Ø609
Ø533 PCD
8X Ø17.5
EQUALLY SPACED
45°
22.5°
A
R179.5
166
50
100
Ø382
A

50
80
B
116
50
100
129.5
20
Ø609

SECTION A-A
(SCALE 1:2)

20
Ø17.5

DETAIL B
(SCALE 2:1)

EX-87

Ø36
Ø100
Ø60
Ø20
Ø40
A   A

Ø60
Ø40
Ø36
Ø20
15
55   13
20
3 x 45°
100
140
185
Ø80
3 x 45°
30
20
Ø60
Ø100
SECTION A-A

P-45

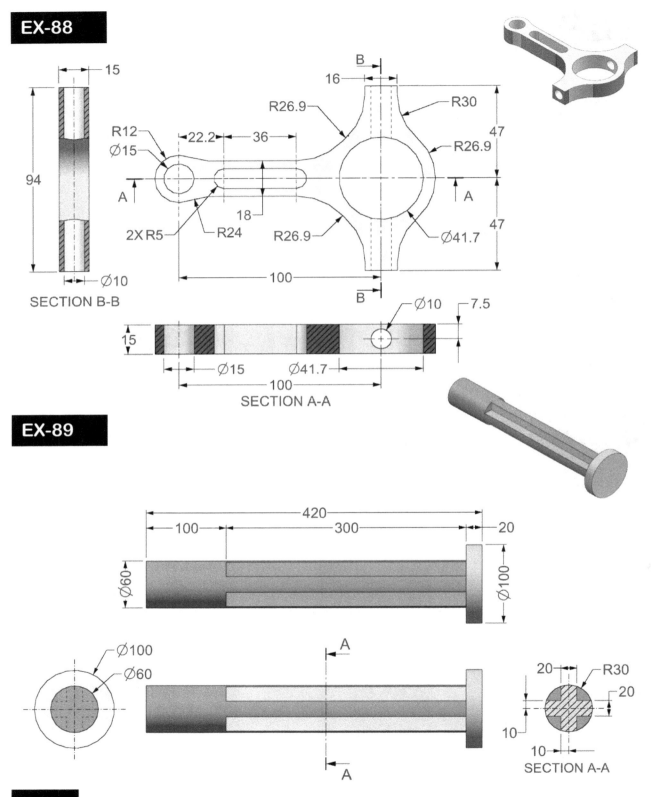

EX-88

SECTION B-B

15
94
∅10

R12
∅15
A
2X R5
R24

22.2
36
18

R26.9
R30
47
R26.9
R26.9
47
100
∅41.7

16
B

SECTION A-A

15
∅15
∅41.7
100
∅10
7.5

EX-89

420
100
300
20
∅60
∅100

∅100
∅60

A
A

20
R30
20
10
10
SECTION A-A

P-46

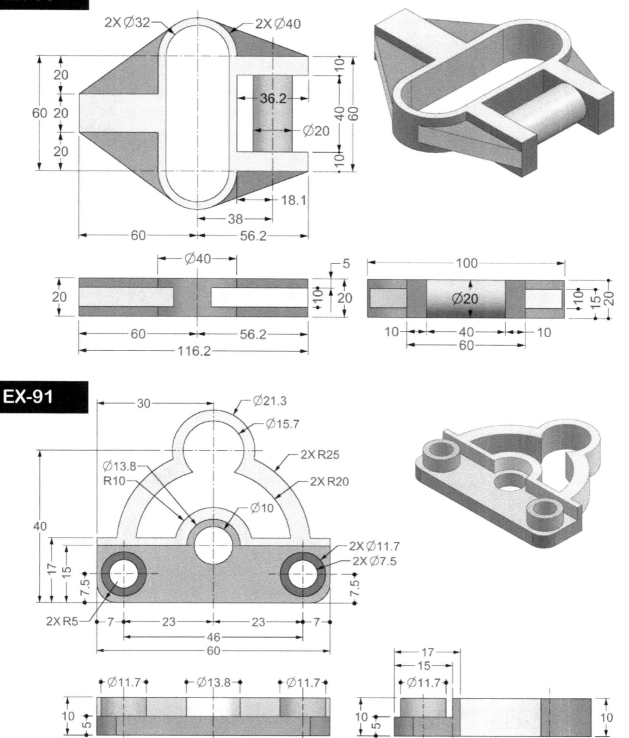

EX-90

2X ⌀32   2X ⌀40
60   20   20   20
36.2   ⌀20
10   40   60   10
18.1
38
60   56.2

⌀40
20
10   20
60   56.2
116.2

100
⌀20
10   15   20
10   40   10
60

EX-91

30   ⌀21.3
⌀15.7
⌀13.8   2X R25
R10   2X R20
⌀10
40
17   15   2X ⌀11.7
7.5   2X ⌀7.5
2X R5   7   23   23   7   7.5
46
60

⌀11.7   ⌀13.8   ⌀11.7
10   5
7   23   23   7
60

17
15
⌀11.7
10   5   10
7.5   25
40

P-47

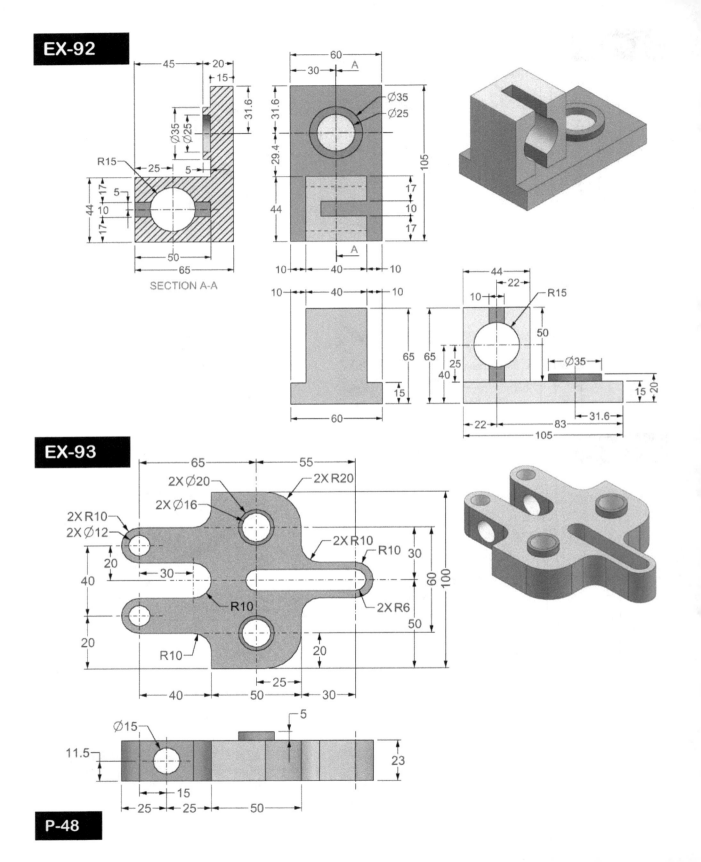

EX-92

SECTION A-A

EX-93

P-48

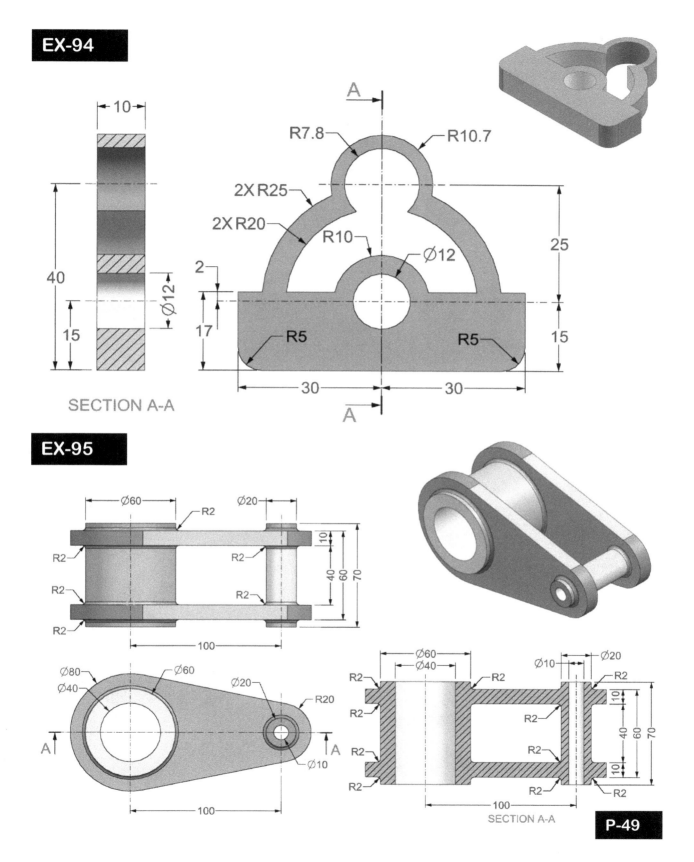

EX-94

10

40

Ø12

15

SECTION A-A

A

R7.8   R10.7

2X R25

2X R20

R10   Ø12

25

2

17

R5   R5

15

30   30

A

EX-95

Ø60   R2   Ø20

R2   R2

R2   R2

10

40

60

70

R2

100

Ø80   Ø60   Ø20   R20

Ø40

A   A

Ø10

100

Ø60   Ø10   Ø20

Ø40

R2   R2   R2

R2   10

R2   40

R2   60

R2   70

R2   10

R2   R2

100

SECTION A-A

P-49

EX-96

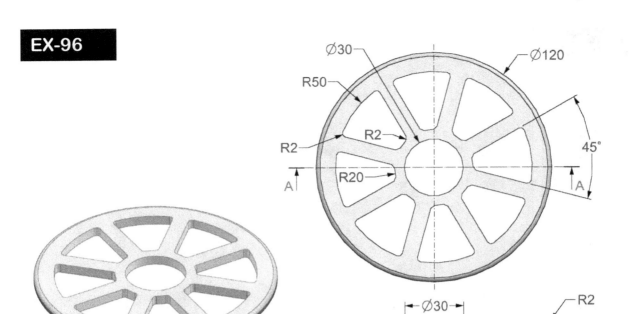

Ø30
Ø120
R50
R2
R2
R20
45°

SECTION A-A
Ø30
Ø120
R2
R2

EX-97

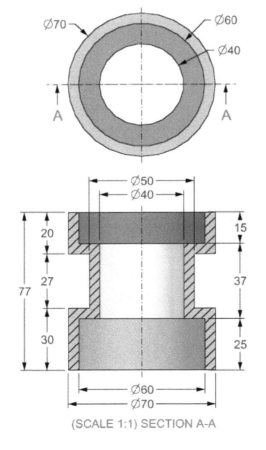
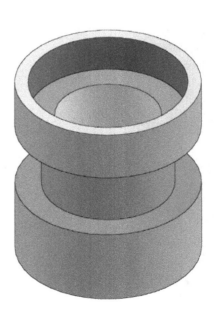

Ø70
Ø60
Ø40

Ø50
Ø40
20
15
27
37
77
30
25
Ø60
Ø70

(SCALE 1:1) SECTION A-A

P-50

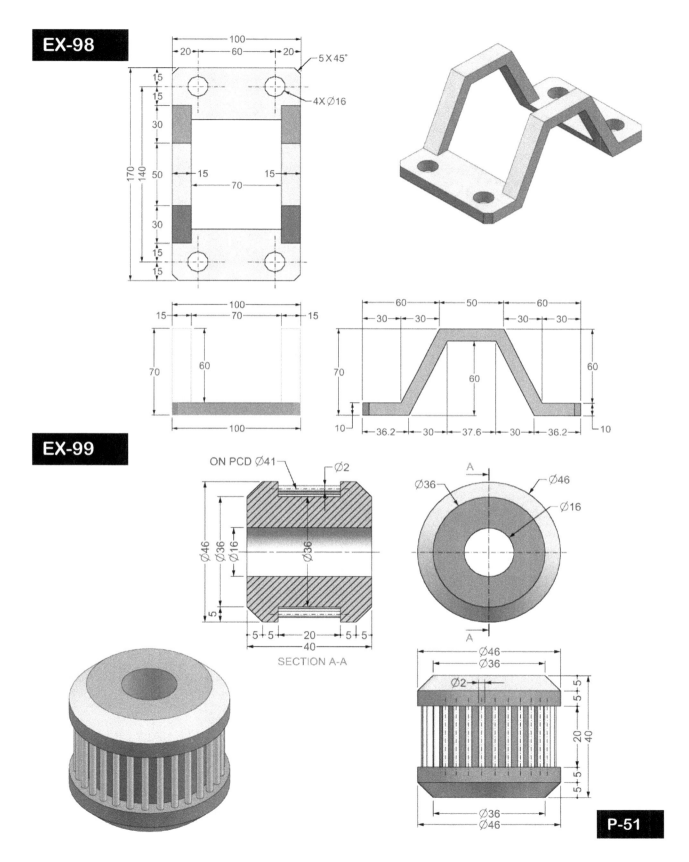

EX-98

EX-99

ON PCD Ø41

SECTION A-A

P-51

EX-100

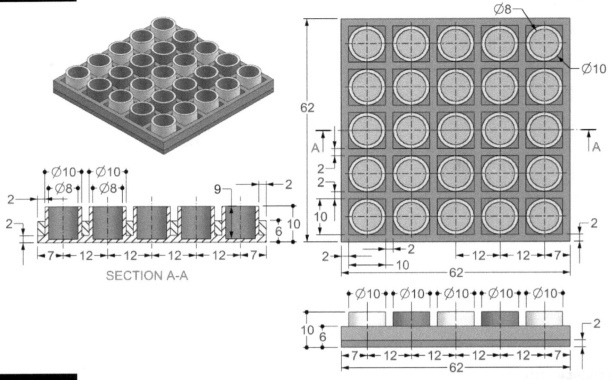

SECTION A-A

EX-101

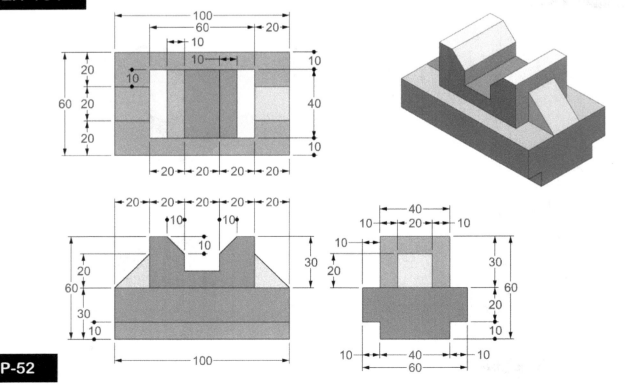

P-52

EX-102

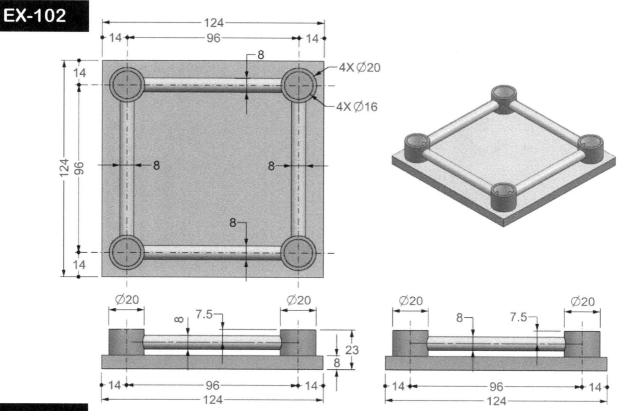

EX-103

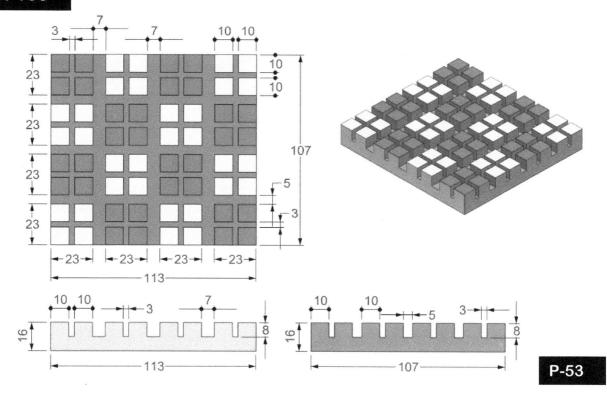

EX-104

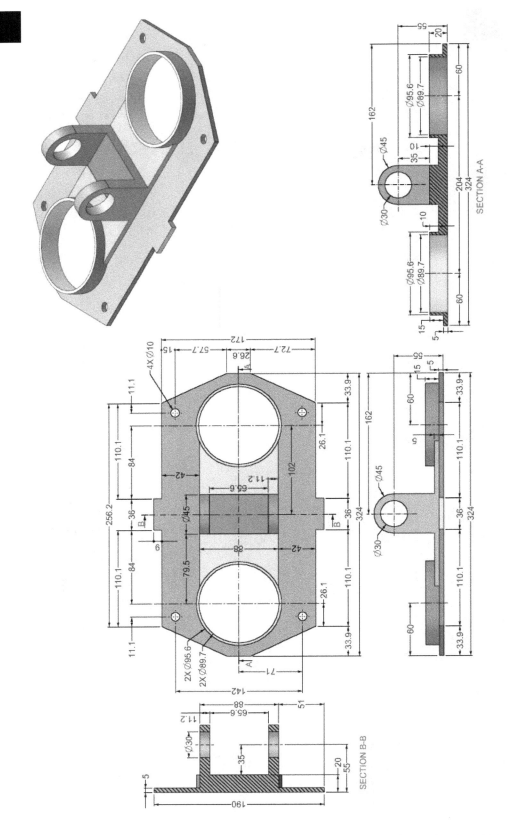

SECTION A-A

SECTION B-B

P-54

EX-105

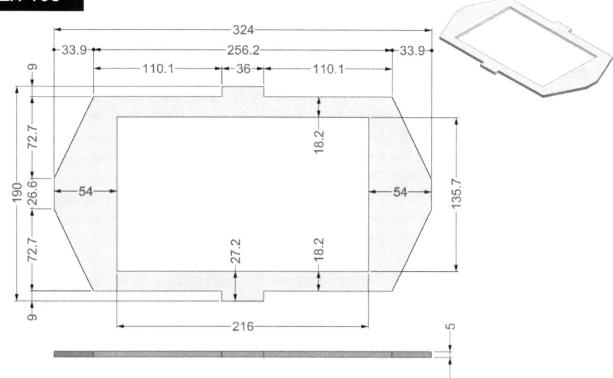

EX-106

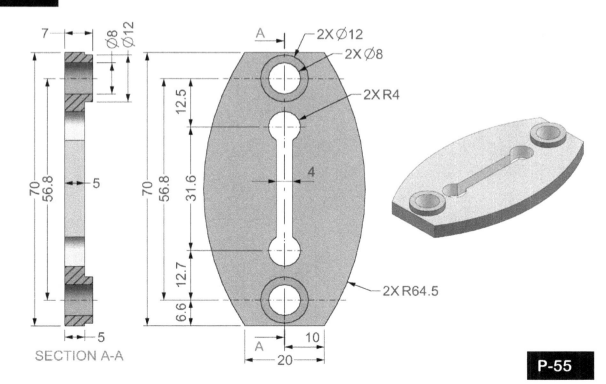

SECTION A-A

EX-107

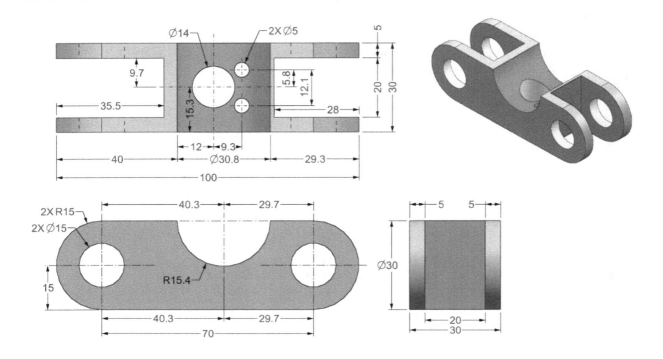

EX-108

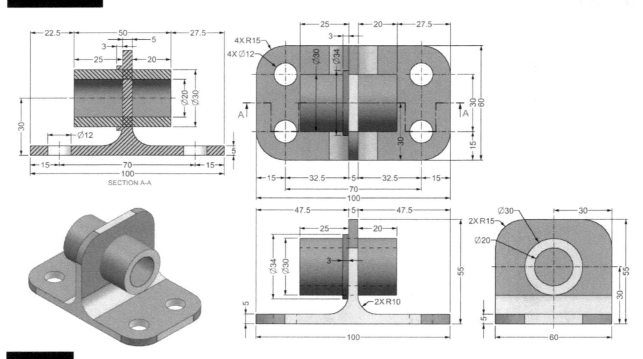

P-56

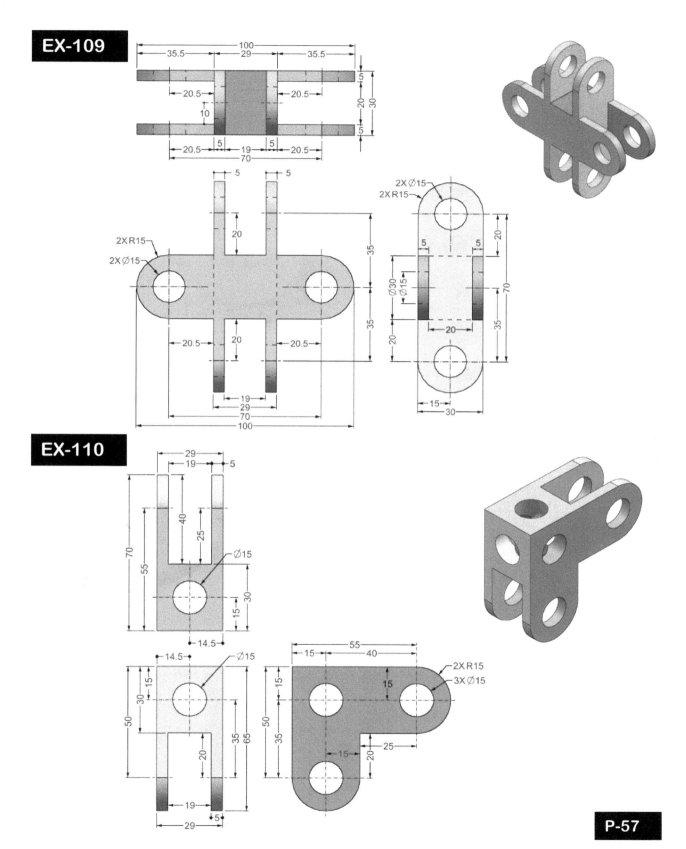

EX-109

EX-110

P-57

EX-111

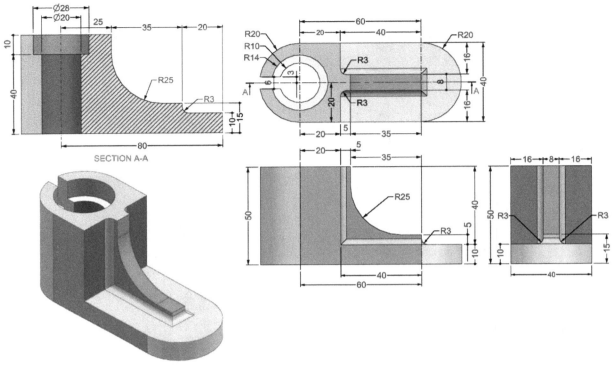

SECTION A-A

EX-112

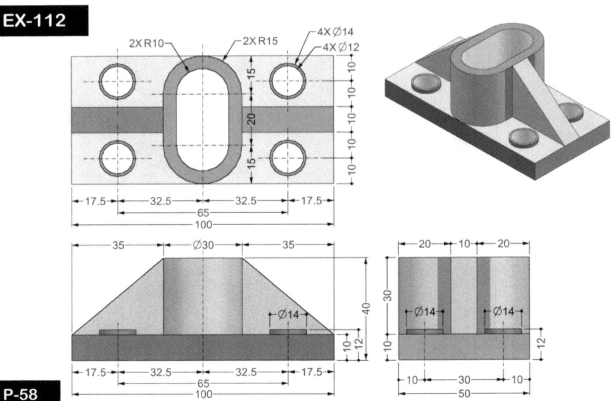

P-58

EX-113

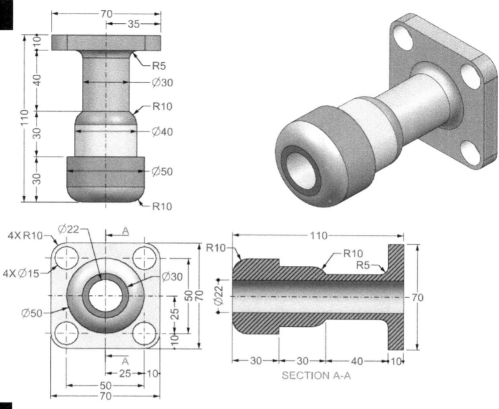

4X R10
Ø22
A
4X Ø15
Ø30
Ø50
50
70
25
10
A
25 10
50
70

R10
110
R10
R5
Ø22
70
30 30 40 10
SECTION A-A

70
35
10
R5
Ø30
40
R10
110
30
Ø40
30
Ø50
R10

EX-114

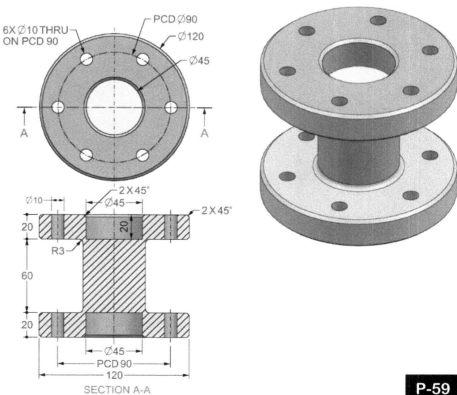

6X Ø10 THRU
ON PCD 90
PCD Ø90
Ø120
Ø45

A
A

Ø10
2 X 45°
Ø45
20
20
2 X 45°
R3
60
20
Ø45
PCD 90
120
SECTION A-A

EX-115

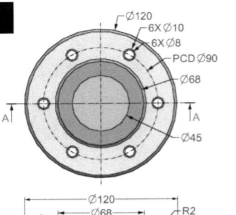

Ø120
6X Ø10
6X Ø8
PCD Ø90
Ø68
Ø45

A | | A

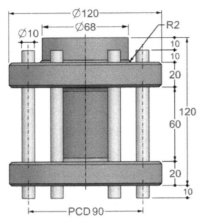

Ø120
Ø68
R2
Ø10
10
10
20
120
60
20
10
PCD 90

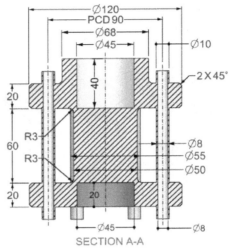

Ø120
PCD 90
Ø68
Ø45
Ø10
2 X 45°
40
20
20
R3
60
Ø8
Ø55
R3
Ø50
20
20
Ø45
Ø8

SECTION A-A

EX-116

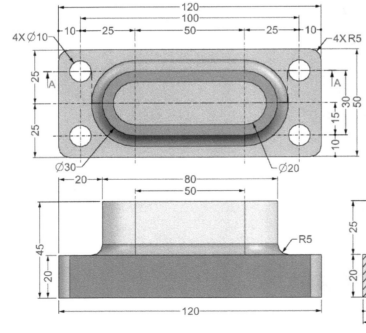

120
100
10
25
50
25
10
4X Ø10
4X R5
25
A
A
30
50
25
15
10
Ø30
Ø20

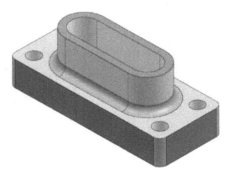

20
80
50
45
R5
20
120

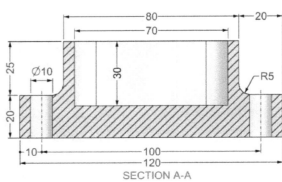

80
20
70
25
Ø10
30
R5
20
10
100
120

SECTION A-A

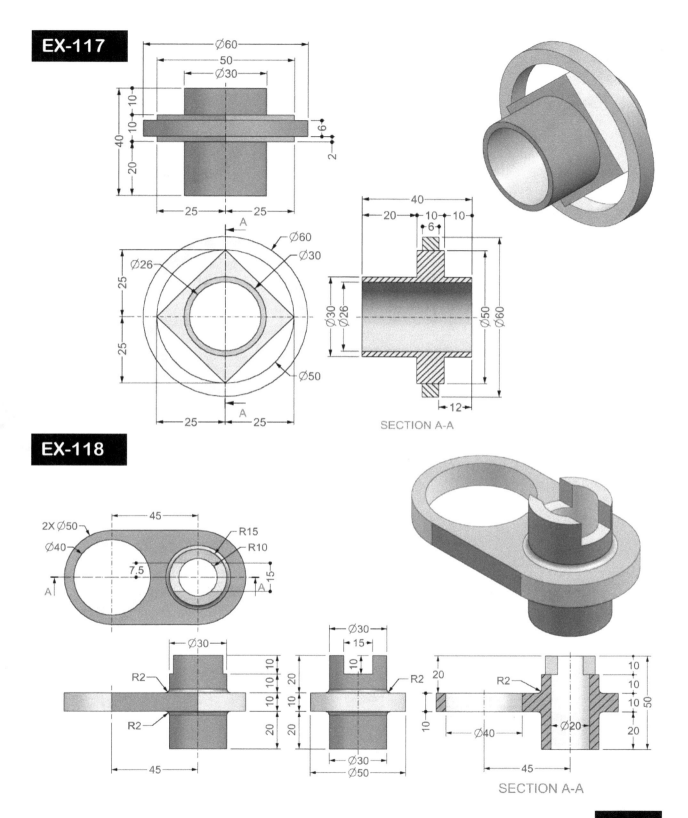

EX-117

⌀60
50
⌀30
10
10
40
20
6
2
25 25
A
⌀26
⌀60
⌀30
25
25
⌀50
25 25
A

40
20 10 10
6
⌀30
⌀26
⌀50
⌀60
12

SECTION A-A

EX-118

2X ⌀50
45
R15
R10
⌀40
7.5
15
A
A

⌀30
R2
10 10
10 10
R2
20
45

⌀30
15
10
20
10
20
R2
⌀30
⌀50

20
R2
10
10
10
20
10
50
⌀40
⌀20
45

SECTION A-A

P-61

EX-119

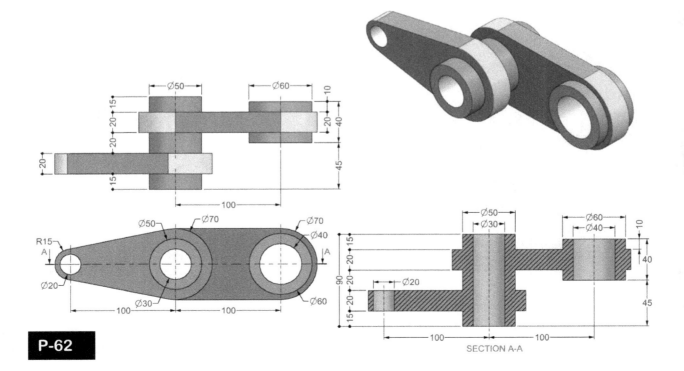

Ø190
Ø55

2X R20
Ø140
70
2X R25
25
50
Ø55
Ø75
Ø100
Ø180
Ø190
SECTION A-A

A
R25
25
50
Ø75
Ø190

Ø75
Ø190
Ø55
Ø180
Ø100

EX-120

Ø50
Ø60
10
15
20
20
20
40
20
15
20
100

Ø50
Ø70
Ø70
Ø40
R15
A
A
Ø20
Ø30
Ø60
100
100

Ø50
Ø30
Ø60
Ø40
10
15
20
20
90
20
Ø20
40
15
45
100
100
SECTION A-A

P-62

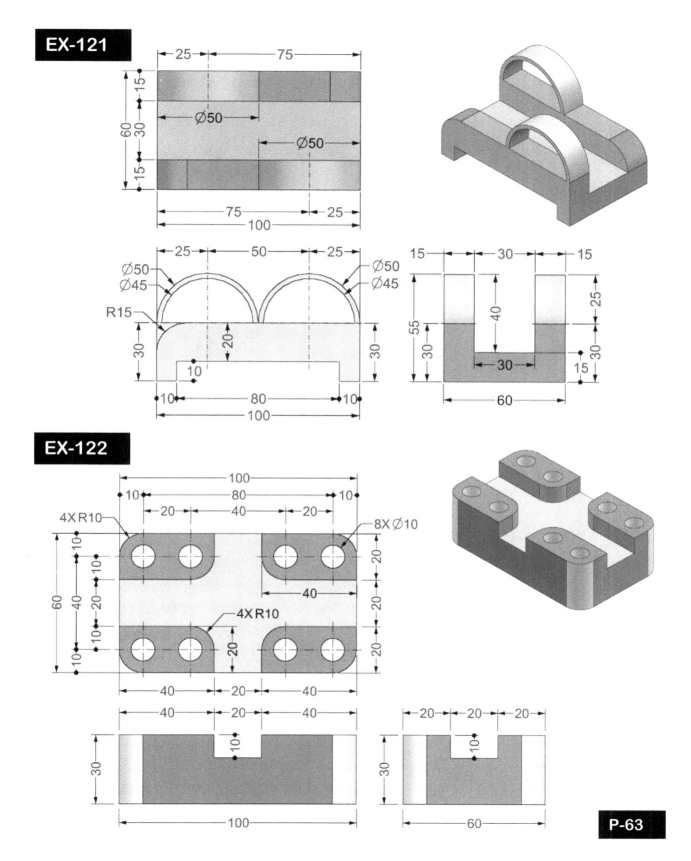

EX-121

EX-122

EX-123

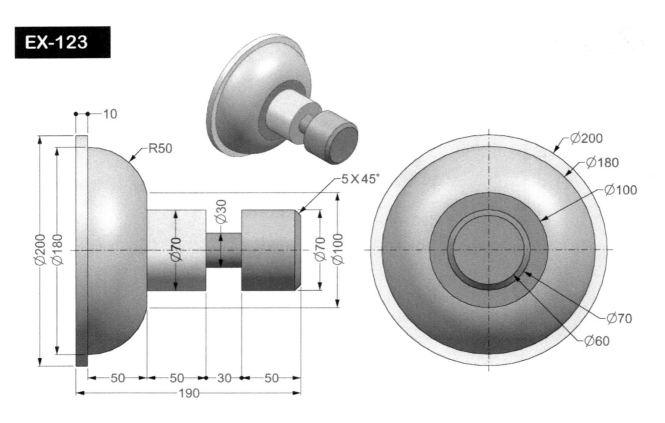

10
R50
5 X 45°
Ø30
Ø70
Ø70
Ø100
Ø200
Ø180
50 50 30 50
190

Ø200
Ø180
Ø100
Ø70
Ø60

EX-124

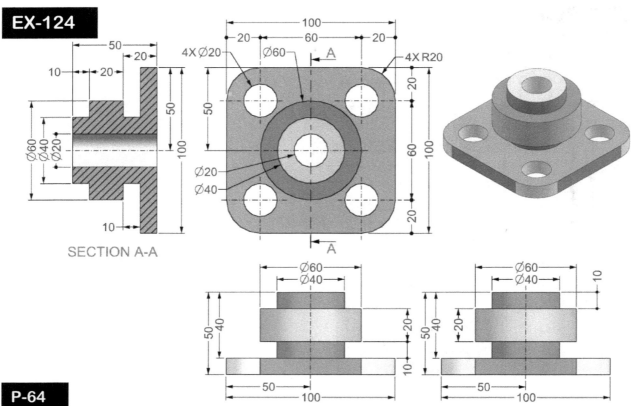

50
20
10 20
Ø60
Ø40
Ø20
50
100
10
SECTION A-A

100
20 60 20
4X Ø20
Ø60
A
4X R20
50
20
60
100
Ø20
Ø40
20
A

Ø60
Ø40
50
40
20
10
50
100

Ø60
Ø40
10
50
40
20
50
100

EX-125

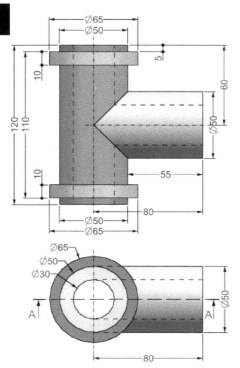

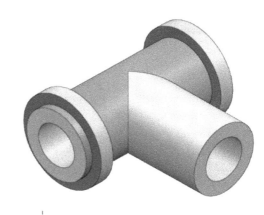

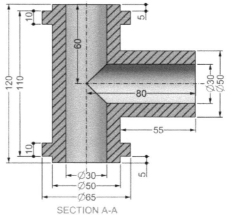

SECTION A-A

EX-126

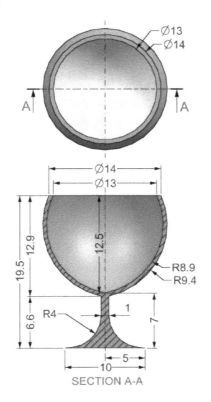

SECTION A-A

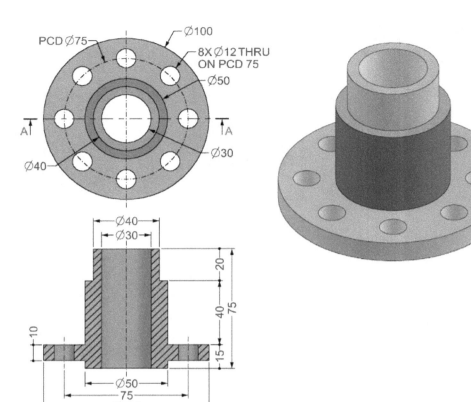

PCD ⌀75

⌀100

8X ⌀12 THRU
ON PCD 75

⌀50

A

A

⌀40

⌀30

⌀40

⌀30

20

40

75

10

15

⌀50

75

⌀100

SECTION A-A

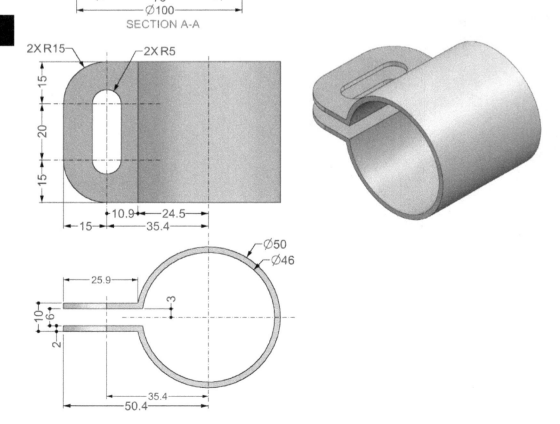

2X R15

2X R5

15

20

15

15

10.9

24.5

35.4

⌀50

⌀46

25.9

3

10

6

2

35.4

50.4

EX-129

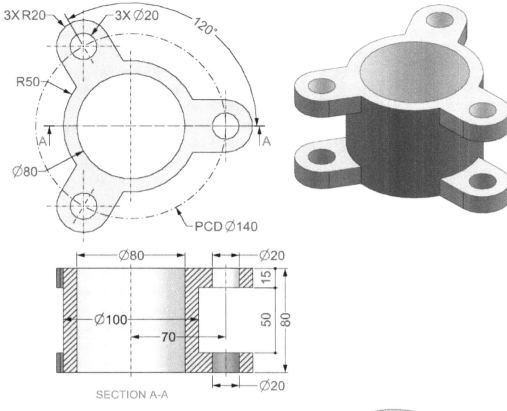

3X R20
3X Ø20
120°
R50
Ø80
PCD Ø140

Ø80
Ø20
15
Ø100
50
80
70
Ø20

SECTION A-A

EX-130

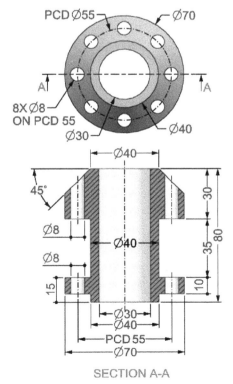

PCD Ø55
Ø70
8X Ø8
ON PCD 55
Ø30
Ø40

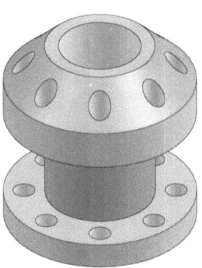

Ø40
45°
30
Ø8
Ø40
80
Ø8
35
15
10
Ø30
Ø40
PCD 55
Ø70

SECTION A-A

EX-131

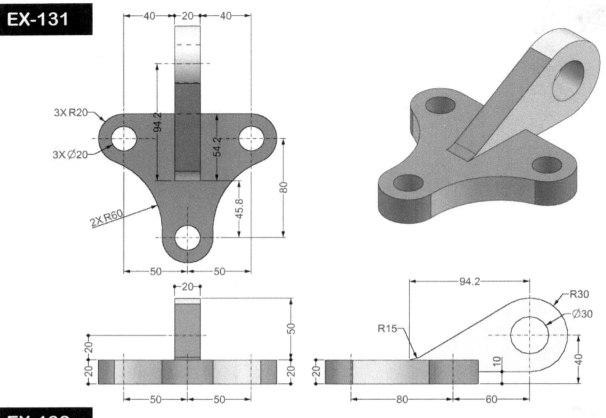

3X R20
3X Ø20
2X R60

40 20 40
94.2
54.2
45.8
80
50 50

20
50
20
20
50 50
20

94.2
R30
Ø30
R15
10
40
20
80 60

EX-132

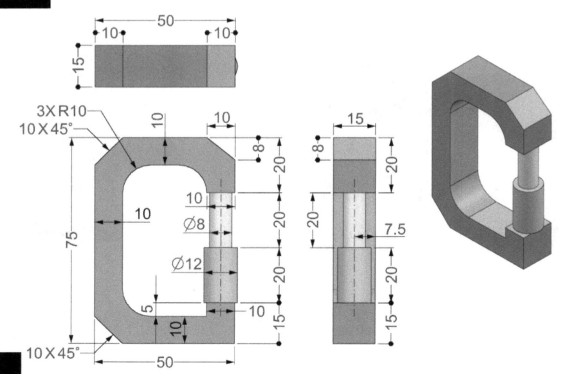

50
10 10
15

3X R10
10 X 45°
10
10
8
20
10
Ø8
20
75
10
Ø12
20
5
10
10
50

15
8
20
20
20
7.5
15

10 X 45°

P-68

EX-133

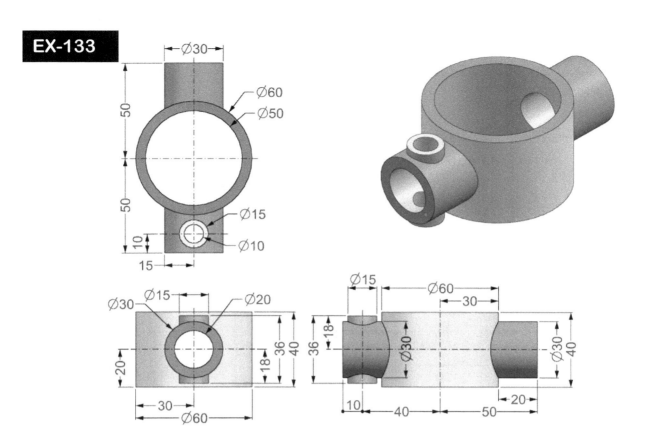

EX-134

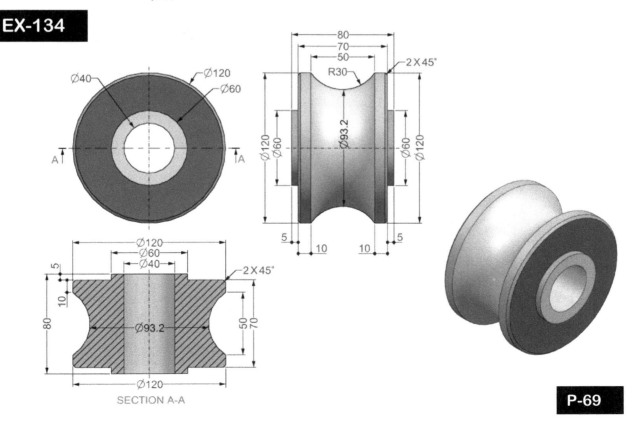

SECTION A-A

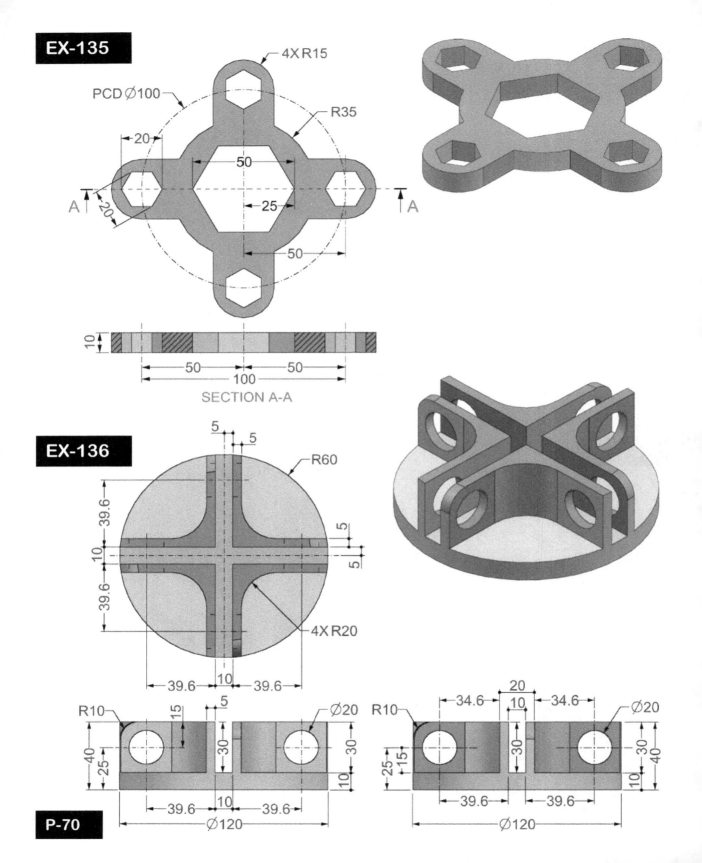

EX-135

4X R15

PCD ⌀100

R35

20

50

25

A

20

A

50

10

50 — 50

100

SECTION A-A

EX-136

5 5

R60

39.6

10

39.6

4X R20

39.6 10 39.6

R10

15

5

⌀20

40

25

30

30

10

39.6 10 39.6

⌀120

R10

20

34.6 10 34.6

⌀20

25

15

30

30

40

10

39.6 39.6

⌀120

P-70

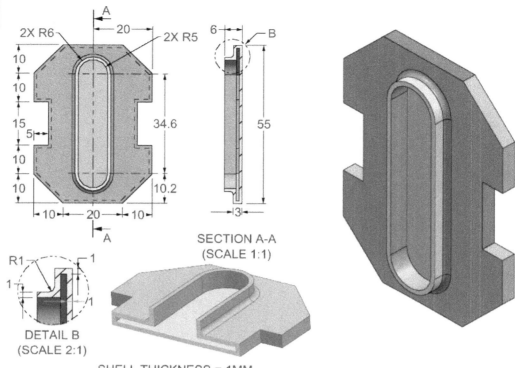

EX-137

2X R6
20
2X R5
10
10
15
5
10
10
34.6
10.2
6
B
55
3
10
20
10

A
A

SECTION A-A
(SCALE 1:1)

R1
1
1
1
1

DETAIL B
(SCALE 2:1)

SHELL THICKNESS = 1MM
ALL INSIDE WALL THICKNESS

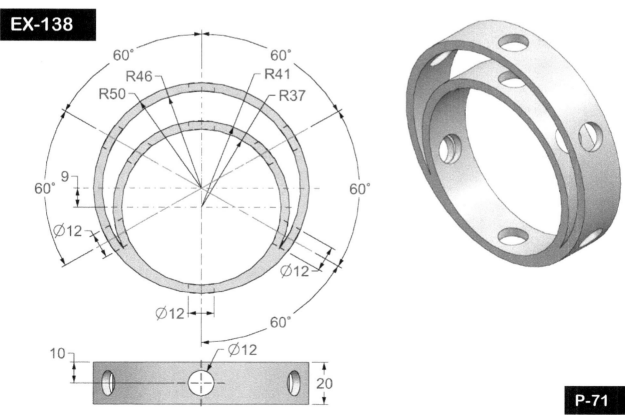

EX-138

60°
60°
R46
R41
R50
R37
60°
9
60°
Ø12
Ø12
Ø12
60°
10
Ø12
20

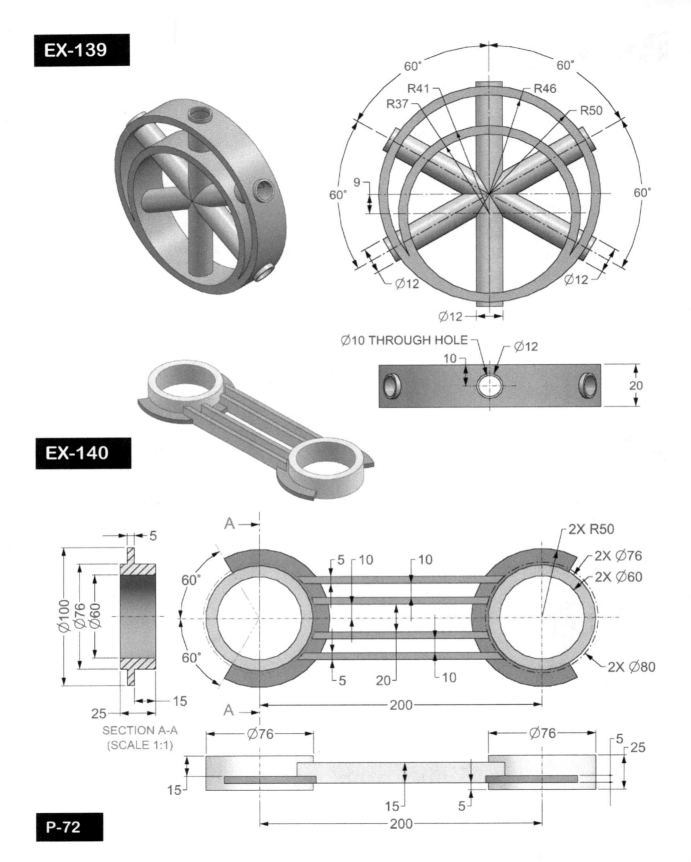

EX-139

60° 60°
R41 R46
R37 R50
60° 60°
9
60°
Ø12 Ø12
Ø12

Ø10 THROUGH HOLE Ø12
10
20

EX-140

2X R50
2X Ø76
2X Ø60
5 10 10
60°
Ø100
Ø76
Ø60
60°
5 20 10
2X Ø80
15
A
25 A
200

SECTION A-A
(SCALE 1:1)

Ø76 Ø76
5
25
15
15 5
200

P-72

EX-141

∅100
∅60
∅6
∅120

∅60 ∅6
30
R5
10
R40.7
10
100
50
∅60
20
R5
∅80
R2 R5
30
∅120

EX-142

18 14 15 41.4
15.4
R15
R10
46.8
∅8
∅16.2
8
∅20.4
23.4
∅16.2
26
R6

10 20
15
5

EX-143

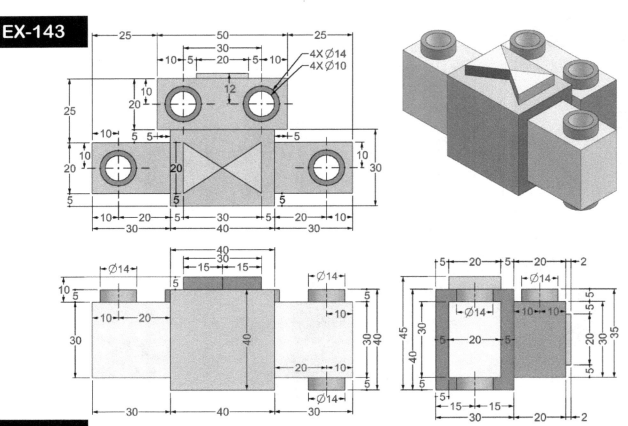

EX-144

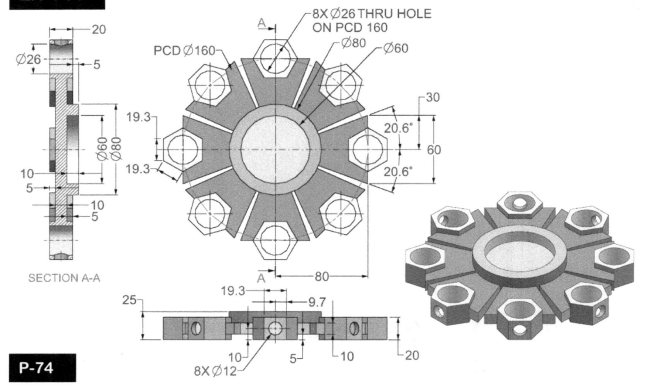

SECTION A-A

8X Ø26 THRU HOLE
ON PCD 160

PCD Ø160

Ø80   Ø60

8X Ø12

P-74

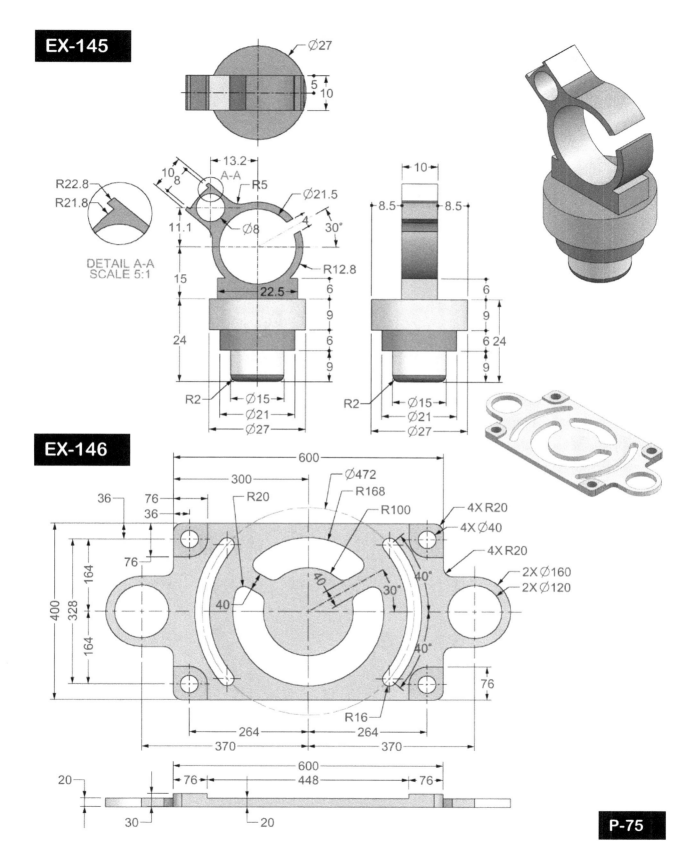

EX-145

∅27

5
10

R22.8
R21.8

DETAIL A-A
SCALE 5:1

13.2
10
8
A-A
R5
∅21.5
∅8
4
30°
11.1
R12.8
15
22.5
6
9
24
6
9
R2
∅15
∅21
∅27

10
8.5
8.5
6
9
6 24
9
R2
∅15
∅21
∅27

EX-146

600
300
∅472
R168
R100
36
76
R20
4X R20
36
4X ∅40
76
4X R20
164
2X ∅160
2X ∅120
400
328
40
40
30°
40°
164
40
40°
76
R16
264
264
370
370

600
20
76
448
76
30
20

P-75

Ø40
120°
Ø20
120°
10
60

R10
Ø40
200
79.6
Ø20
15
60
R15

2X Ø100
2X Ø80
Ø50
R45
R40
Ø30
51.6
A
A
100
100

Ø90
Ø50
10
10
40
15
100
100

Ø90
Ø80
Ø50
Ø30
Ø80
Ø80
15
10
10
40
15
100
100

SECTION A-A

EX-149

∅24
2X R5 — R24
R30
∅41.7
18
∅15
22.2 — 35.9
100
R26.9

100
15
5
∅15
∅24
5
∅41.7
SECTION A-A

EX-150

67.5
17.8
13.3
14.4
10
R16.7
R21.5
R9.6
R4
∅12
R15.7
R6.1
R6.2
2X R19.2
45.9
3.6
19

5
∅12
SECTION A-A

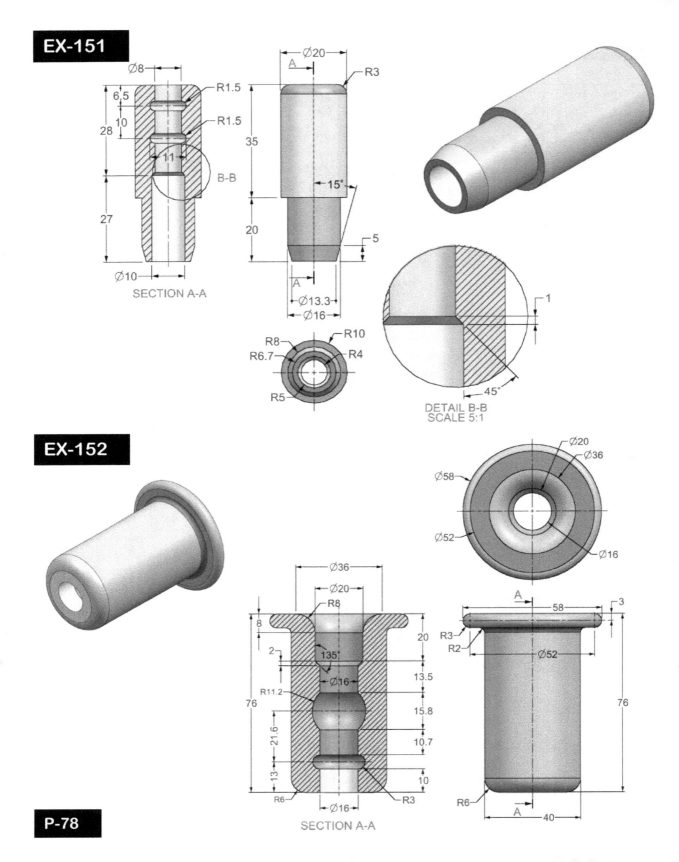

EX-151

Ø8
6,5
10
28
R1.5
R1.5
11
B-B
27
Ø10
SECTION A-A

Ø20
A
R3
35
15°
20
5
A
Ø13.3
Ø16

R8
R10
R6.7
R4
R5

1
45°
DETAIL B-B
SCALE 5:1

EX-152

Ø20
Ø36
Ø58
Ø52
Ø16

Ø36
Ø20
R8
8
2
135°
Ø16
R11.2
76
21.6
13
R6
Ø16
R3
20
13.5
15.8
10.7
10

A
58
3
R3
R2
Ø52
76
R6
A
40
SECTION A-A

P-78

EX-153

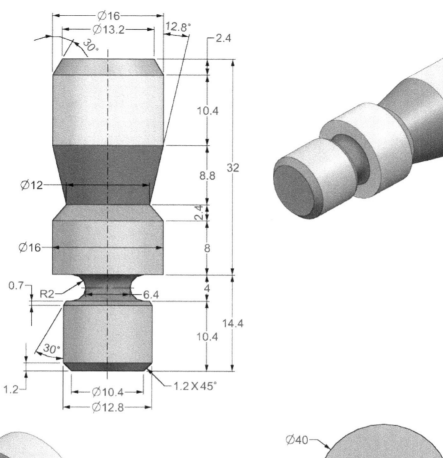

Ø16
Ø13.2
12.8°
30°
2.4
10.4
8.8
32
2.4
Ø12
8
Ø16
4
0.7
R2
6.4
14.4
30°
10.4
1.2
Ø10.4
Ø12.8
1.2 X 45°

EX-154

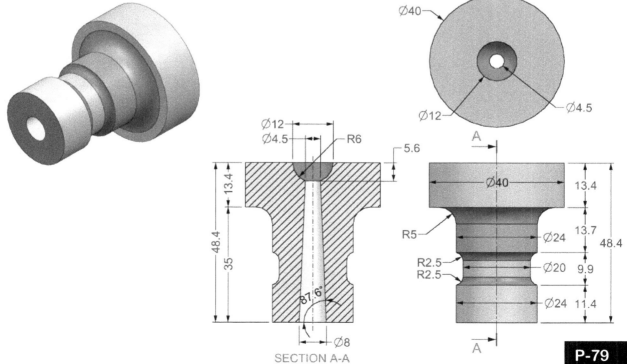

Ø40
Ø12
Ø4.5

Ø12
Ø4.5
R6
5.6
13.4
48.4
35
87.6°
Ø8
SECTION A-A

A
Ø40
13.4
R5
Ø24
13.7
48.4
R2.5
R2.5
Ø20
9.9
Ø24
11.4
A

EX-155

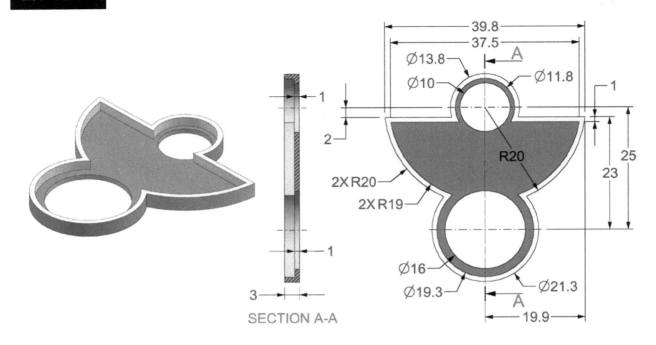

Ø13.8
Ø10
Ø11.8
39.8
37.5
A
R20
2X R20
2X R19
Ø16
Ø19.3
Ø21.3
25
23
1
1
2
1
3
SECTION A-A
19.9

EX-156

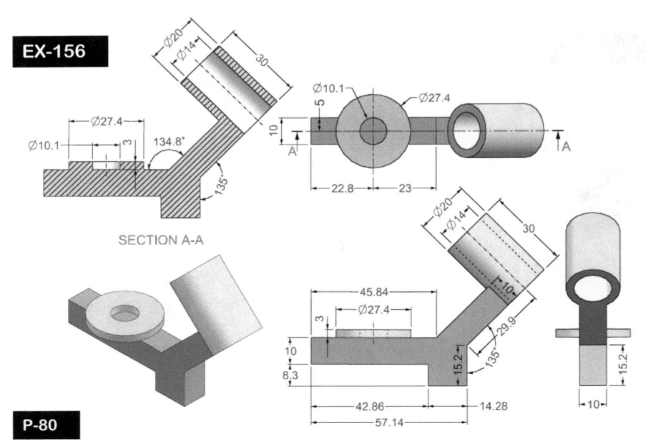

Ø20
Ø14
30
Ø27.4
Ø10.1
3
134.8°
135°
SECTION A-A

Ø10.1
Ø27.4
5
10
A
22.8
23
A

Ø20
Ø14
30
10
29.9
135°
45.84
Ø27.4
3
10
8.3
15.2
42.86
14.28
57.14
15.2
10

P-80

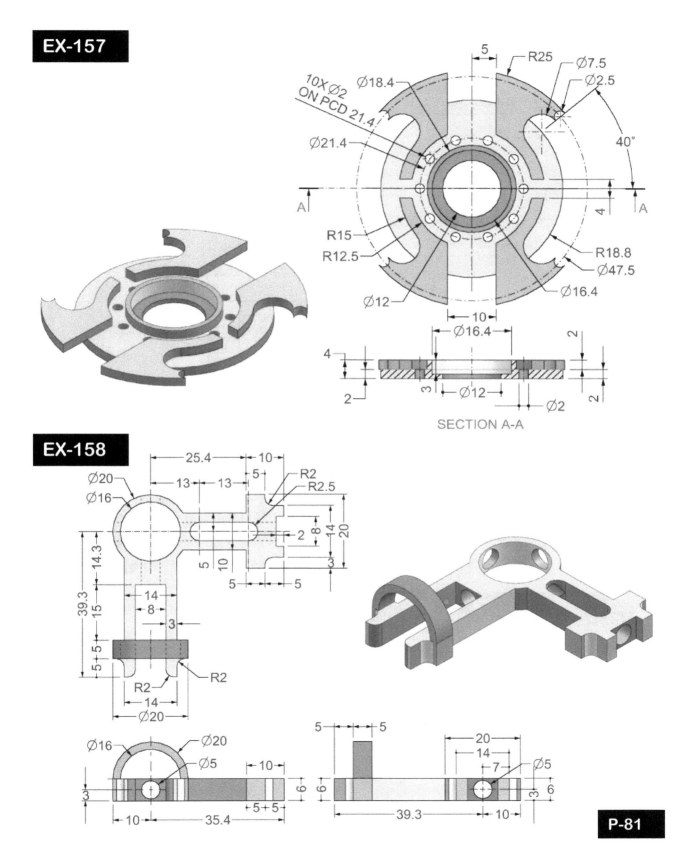

EX-157

10X∅2
ON PCD 21.4
∅18.4
5
R25
∅7.5
∅2.5
∅21.4
40°
R15
R12.5
R18.8
∅47.5
∅16.4
∅12
4
A — A

10
∅16.4
4
2
3
∅12
∅2
2
2

SECTION A-A

EX-158

25.4
10
∅20
∅16
13
13
5
R2
R2.5
2
8
14
20
5
10
3
5
5
14.3
39.3
14
8
15
3
5 5
5 5
R2
R2
14
∅20

∅16
∅20
∅5
10
3
10
35.4
5 5
6

5
5
20
14
7
∅5
6
6
39.3
10
3

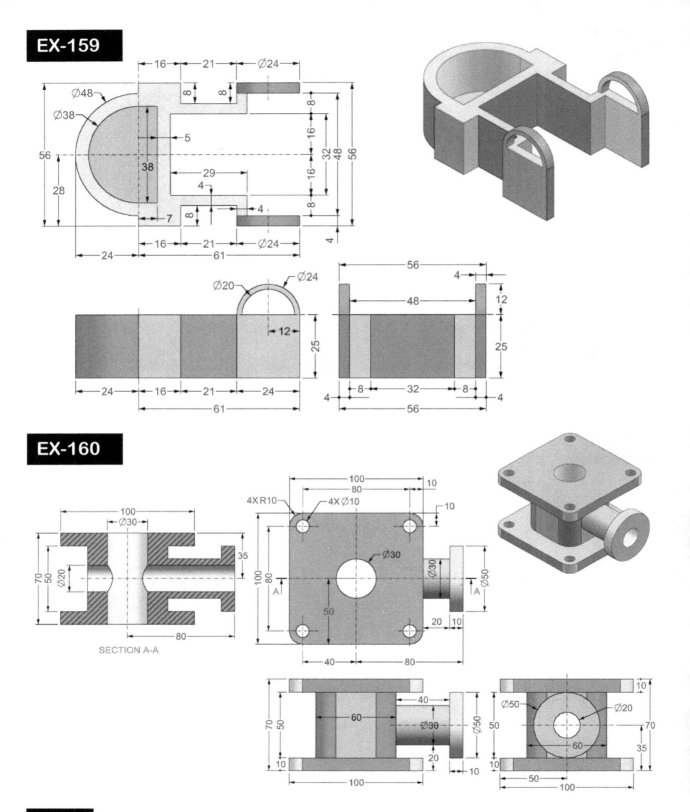

EX-159

EX-160

SECTION A-A

4X R10 4X Ø10

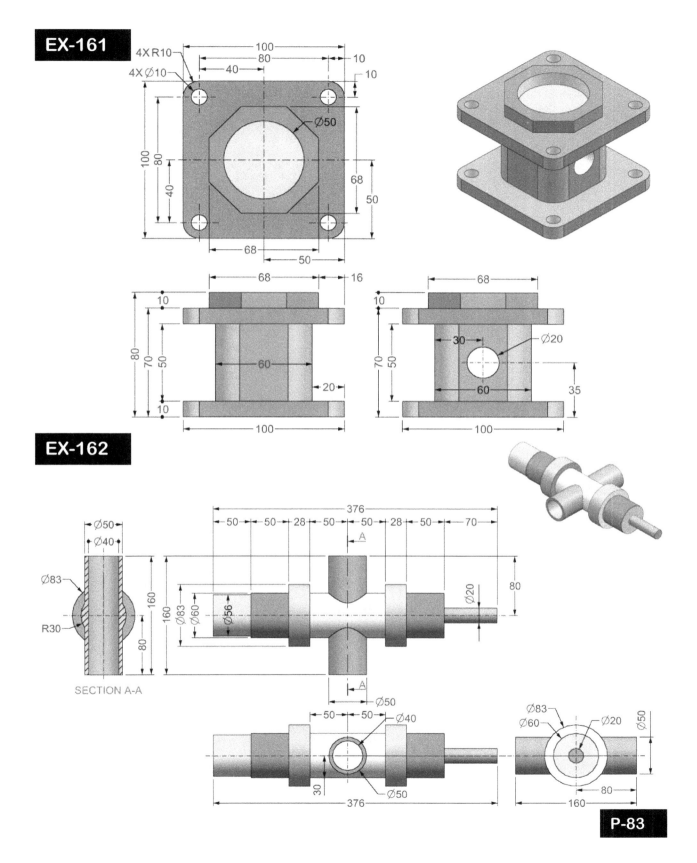

EX-161

EX-162

SECTION A-A

P-83

EX-163

10

Ø20

Ø20

Ø20

20   10

SECTION A-A

A

PCD Ø160
4X Ø20
2X Ø20
2X R10

R100

Ø40

B   B

Ø20
PCD Ø80.5

2X Ø14 THRU HOLES

Ø120

A

TOP VIEW

10

SECTION B-B

20

Ø10

C

Ø20   Ø40

BOTTOM VIEW

C

10

Ø20

Ø20

Ø20

20

SECTION C-C

EX-164

68
28.2
4X Ø10   4X R10

10

Ø50
Ø30

68   28.2   80   100

A   A

40

10

10   40   40   10
80
100

16   68   16

28.2

10 10

80   70   50

Ø18

25   30

60

50

100

100
68
Ø50

10 10

10

50

Ø18

25

50   50

Ø30

100

SECTION A-A

35

P-84

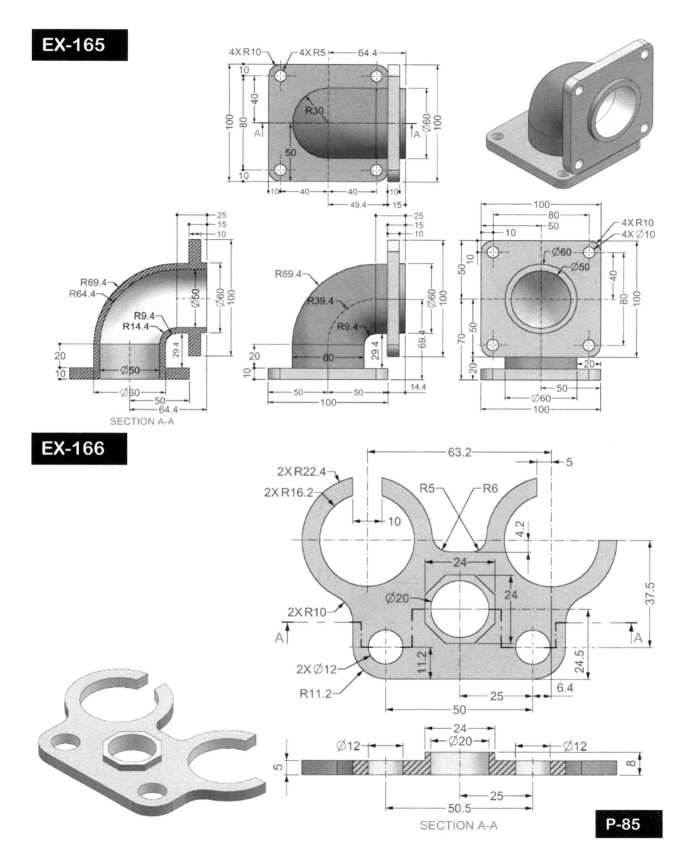

EX-165

EX-166

SECTION A-A

SECTION A-A

P-85

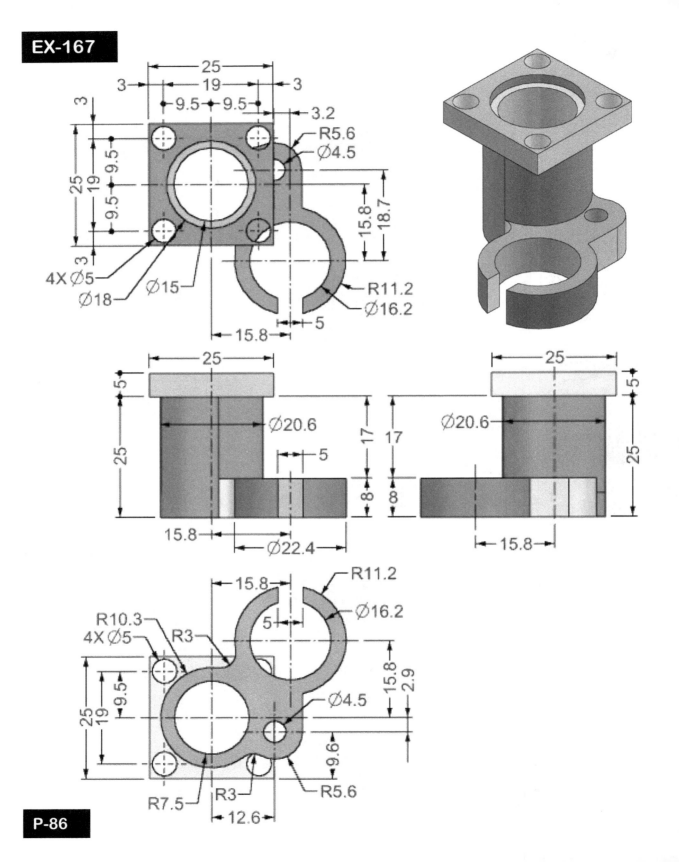

EX-167

P-86

EX-168

PCD Ø95
Ø120
8X Ø14
8X Ø10
ON PCD 95
R35
R25
A
A
6
3

32
30
80 16
32
20
2
Ø70
Ø120

30
Ø14
Ø10
16 20
Ø50
Ø70
PCD 95
Ø120

SECTION A-A

EX-169

Ø70
Ø40
20
R5
40
Ø28
Ø40
50
130
70
200

Ø70
R2
R60
Ø80
R5
30
21.3
50
140
40
80
Ø28
Ø40
30
10
50
80
70

Ø70
15
40
15
10
30
80
Ø28
Ø40
15
15
70
30
10
35
Ø70

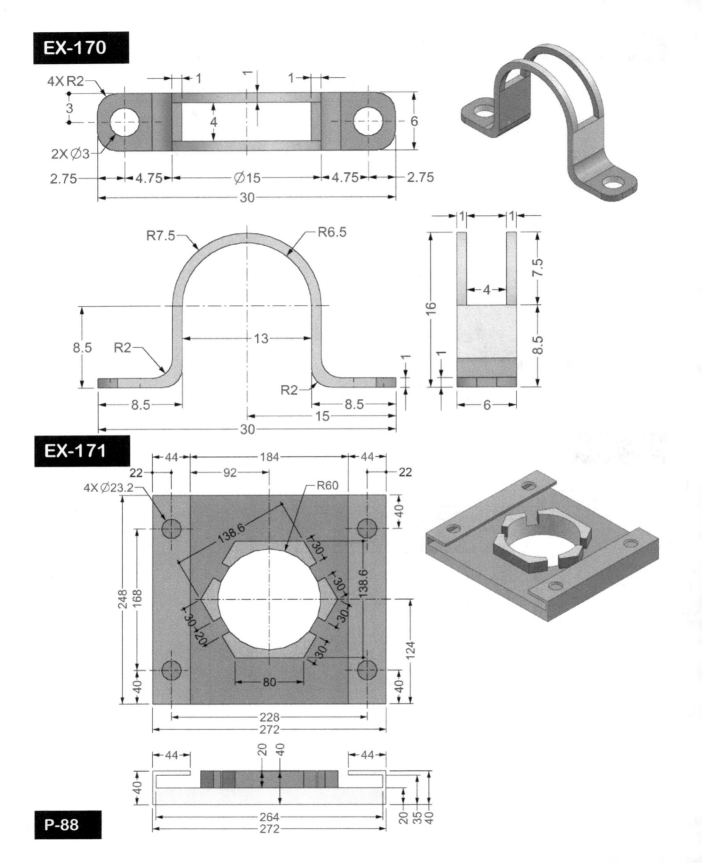

EX-170

4X R2
3
2X Ø3
2.75
4.75
Ø15
4.75
2.75
30
1
1
1
4
6

R7.5
R6.5
R2
8.5
13
R2
8.5
15
8.5
30
1

1
1
16
7.5
4
8.5
1
6

EX-171

44
184
44
22
92
22
4X Ø23.2
R60
138.6
30
30
40
248
168
138.6
30
30-20
30
124
40
80
40
228
272

44
20
40
44
40
20
35
40
264
272

P-88

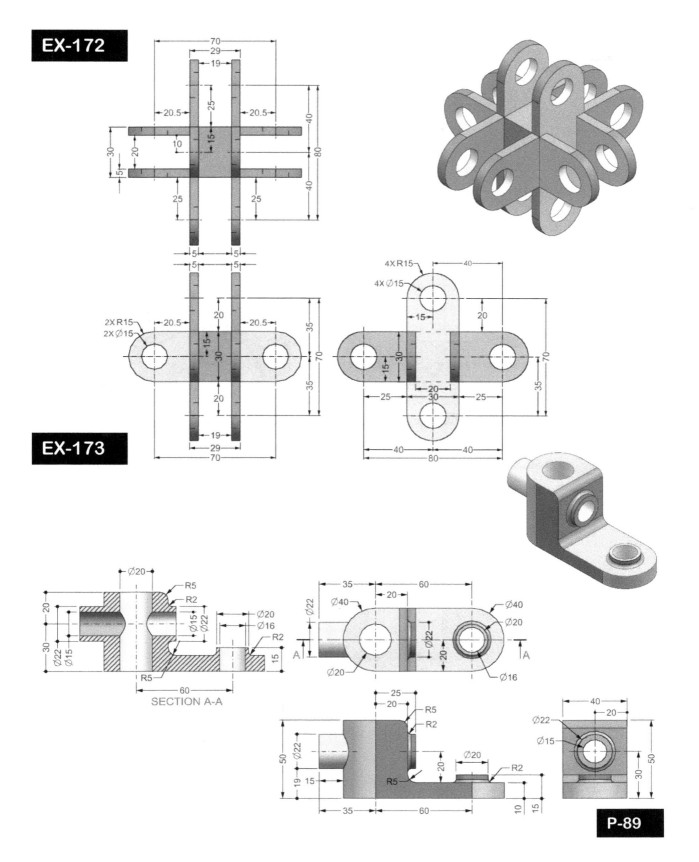

EX-172

EX-173

2X R15
2X Ø15

4X R15
4X Ø15

SECTION A-A

P-89

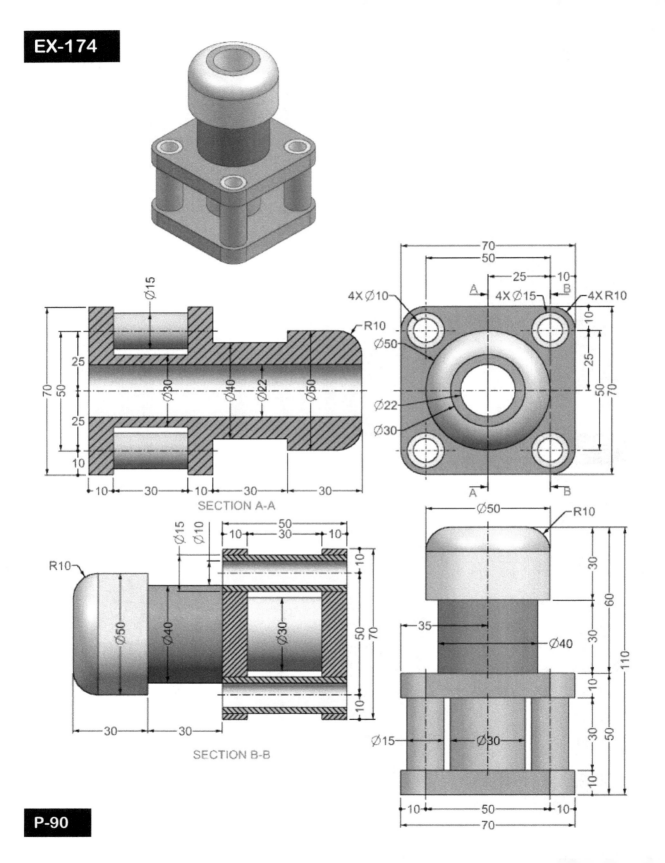

EX-174

SECTION A-A

SECTION B-B

P-90

EX-175

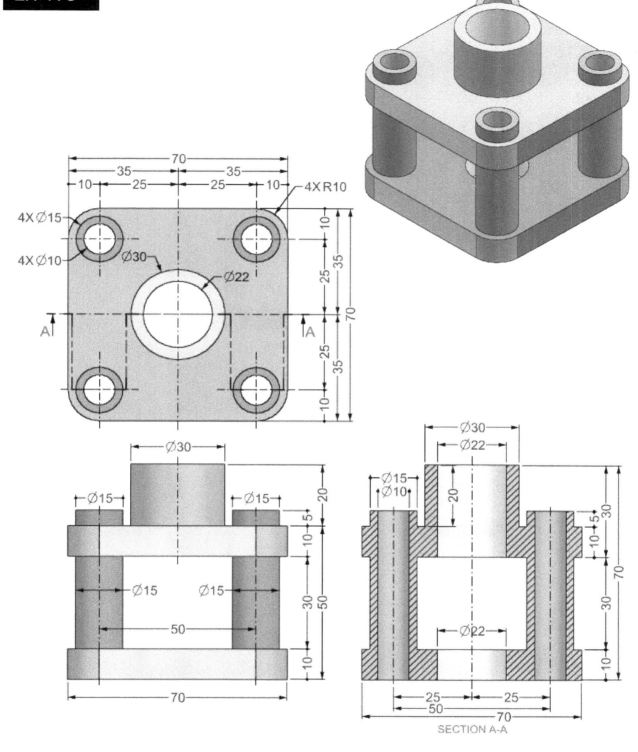

4X Ø15
4X Ø10
Ø30
Ø22
70
35
35
10
25
25
10
4X R10
10
35
25
70
25
35
10
A
A

Ø30
Ø15
Ø15
Ø15
Ø15
50
70
20
5
10
30
50
10

Ø30
Ø22
Ø15
Ø10
20
Ø22
25
25
50
70
5
10
30
30
70
10

SECTION A-A

P-91

EX-176

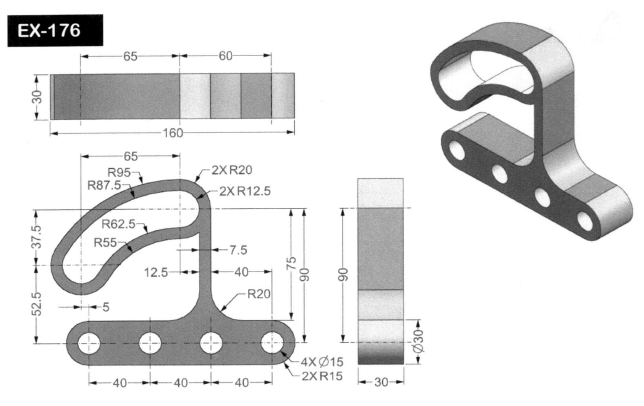

65 · 60

30

160

65

R95
R87.5
2X R20
2X R12.5

R62.5
R55

37.5

7.5

12.5 · 40

52.5

5

R20

90

75

90

∅30

4X ∅15
2X R15

40 · 40 · 40

30

EX-177

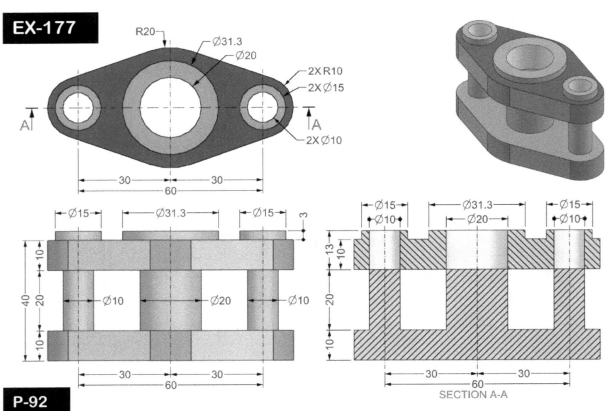

R20

∅31.3
∅20

2X R10
2X ∅15

A

A

2X ∅10

30 · 30

60

∅15 · ∅31.3 · ∅15

3

10

40

20

∅10 · ∅20 · ∅10

10

30 · 30

60

∅15 · ∅31.3 · ∅15
∅10 · ∅20 · ∅10

13
10

20

10

30 · 30

60

SECTION A-A

P-92

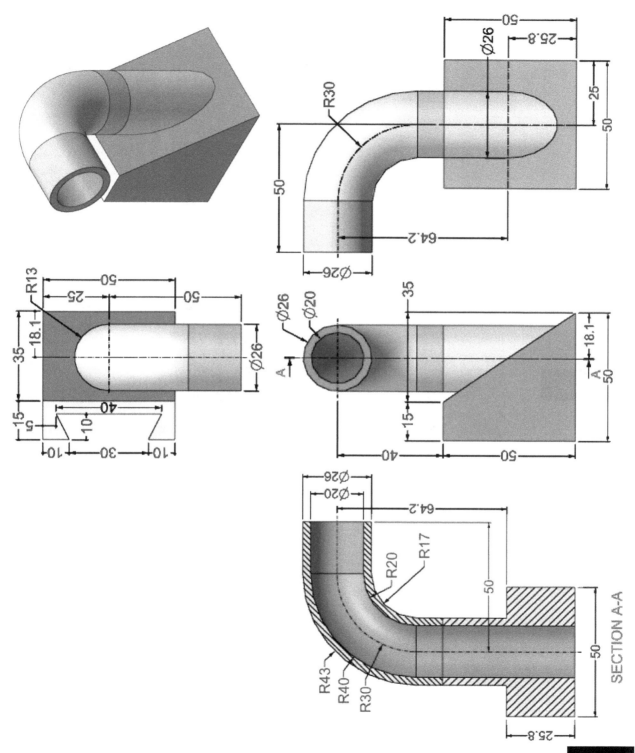

R30
Ø26
50
25
25.8
50
64.2
Ø26

R13
R30
50
25
50
35
18.1
Ø26
40
15
5
10
10
30
10

Ø26
Ø20
35
A
18.1
A
50
15
40
50

Ø26
Ø20
64.2
R20
R17
50
R43
R40
R30
50
25.8
SECTION A-A

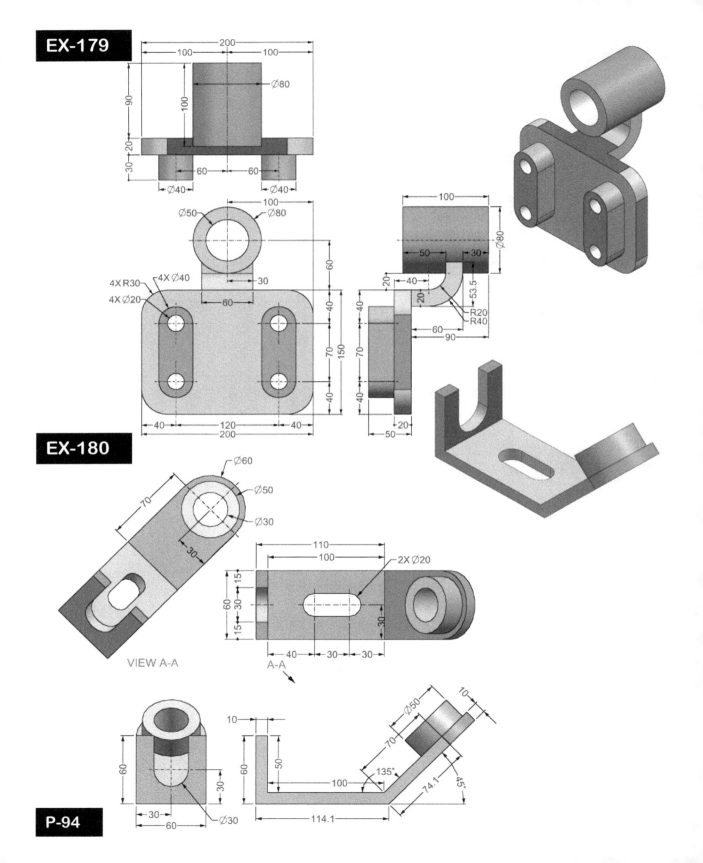

EX-179

EX-180

VIEW A-A

A-A

P-94

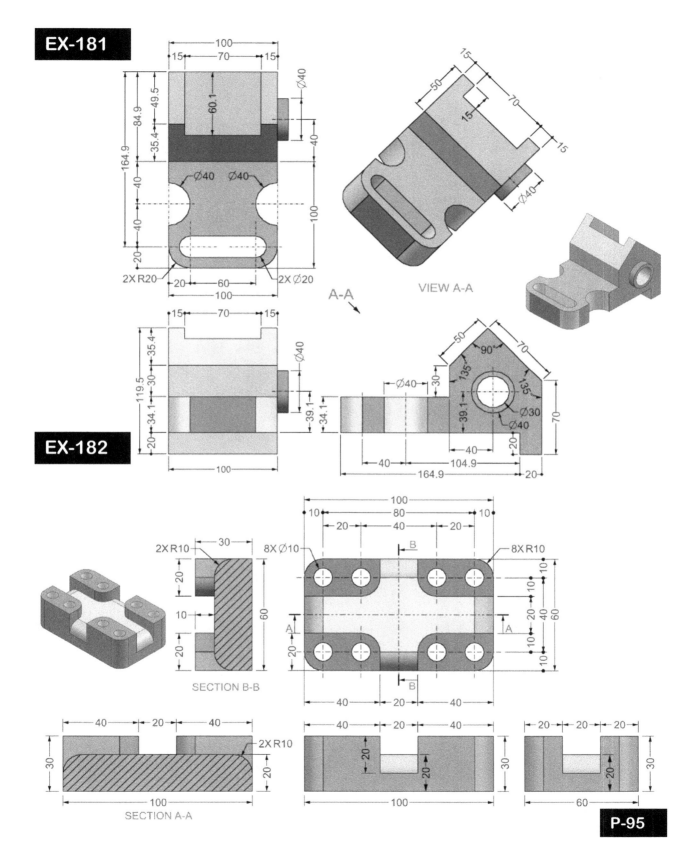

EX-181

EX-182

A-A

VIEW A-A

SECTION B-B

SECTION A-A

P-95

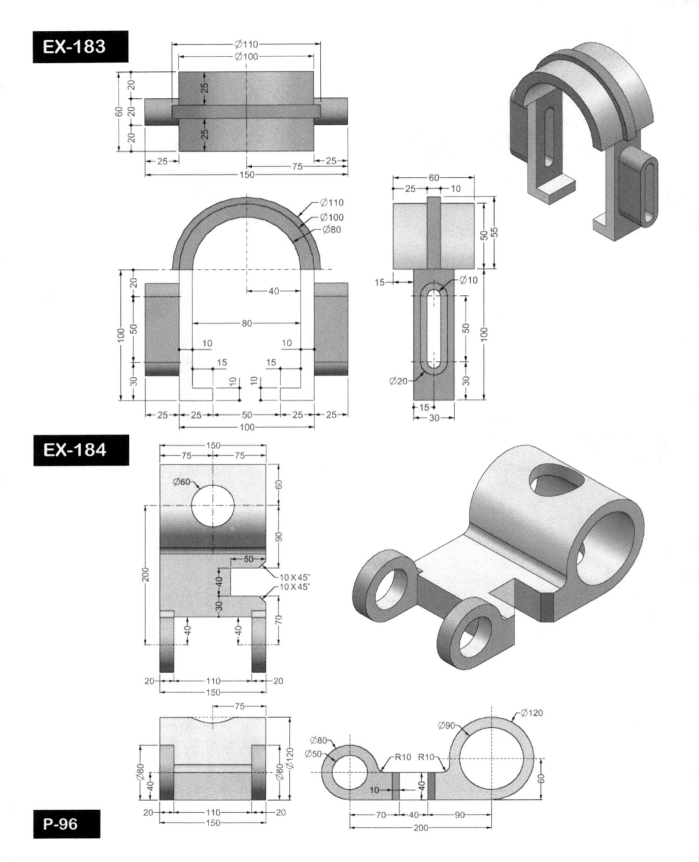

EX-183

Ø110
Ø100
20
20
25
60
20
25
25
75
25
150

Ø110
Ø100
Ø80
20
40
100
50
80
10
10
15
15
30
10
10
25 25 50 25 25
100

60
25 10
50
55
15
Ø10
50
100
Ø20
30
15
30

EX-184

150
75 75
Ø60
60
90
200
50
10 X 45°
40
10 X 45°
30
70
40 40
20 110 20
150

75
Ø80
Ø120
40
Ø80
20 110 20
150

Ø90
Ø120
Ø80
Ø50
R10 R10
10
40
60
70 40 90
200

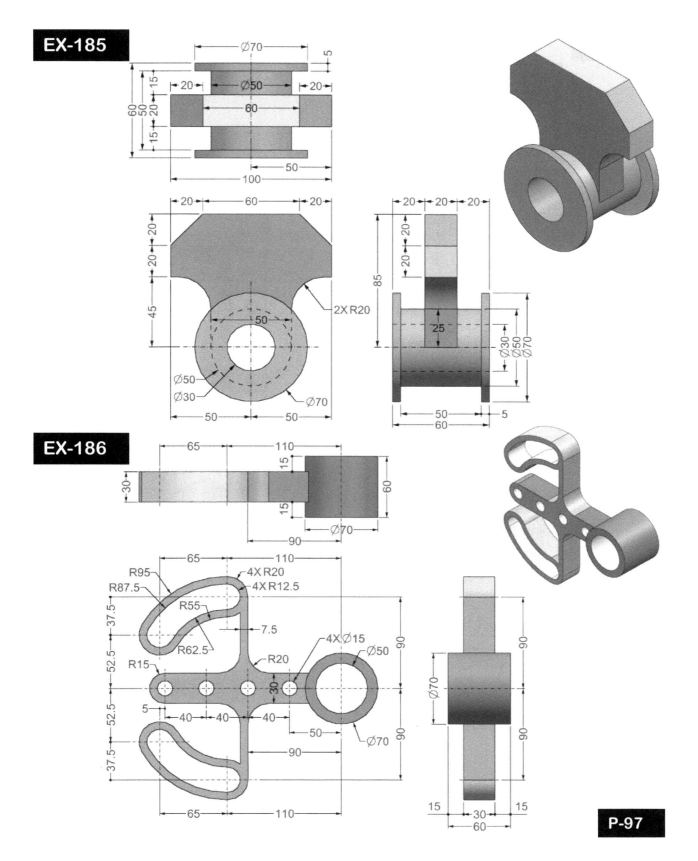

EX-185

EX-186

P-97

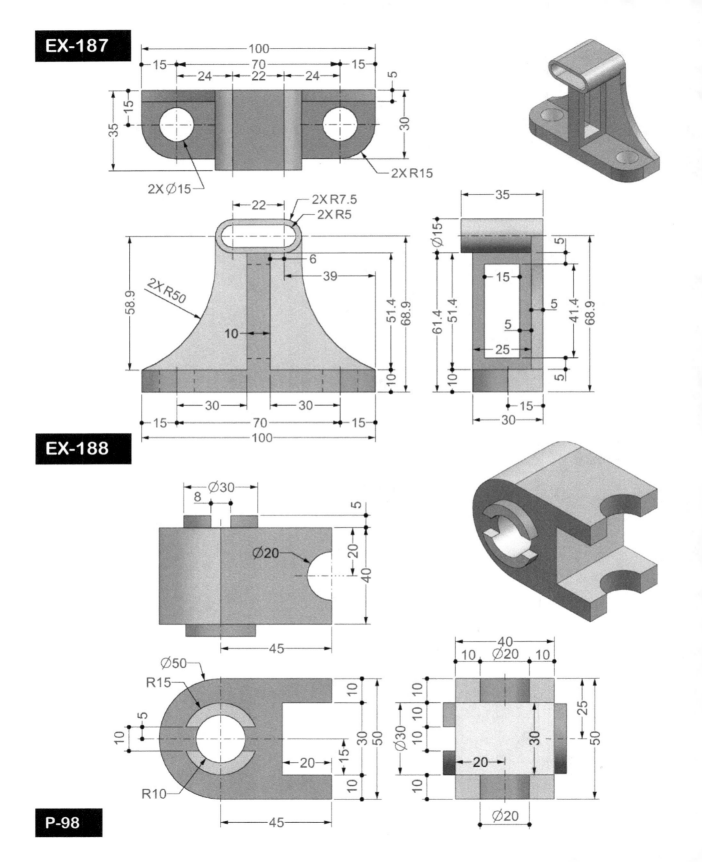

EX-187

EX-188

P-98

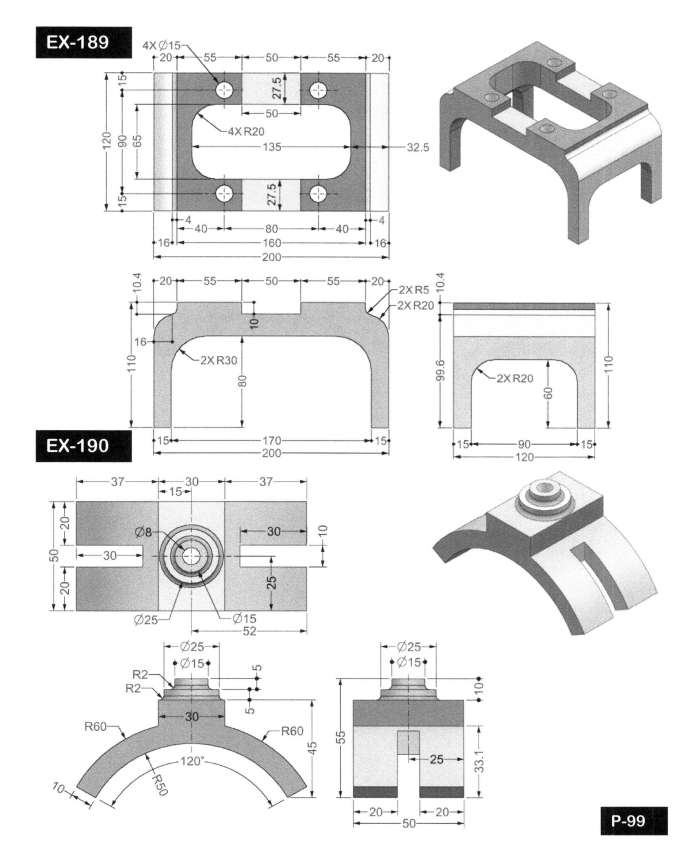

EX-189

EX-190

P-99

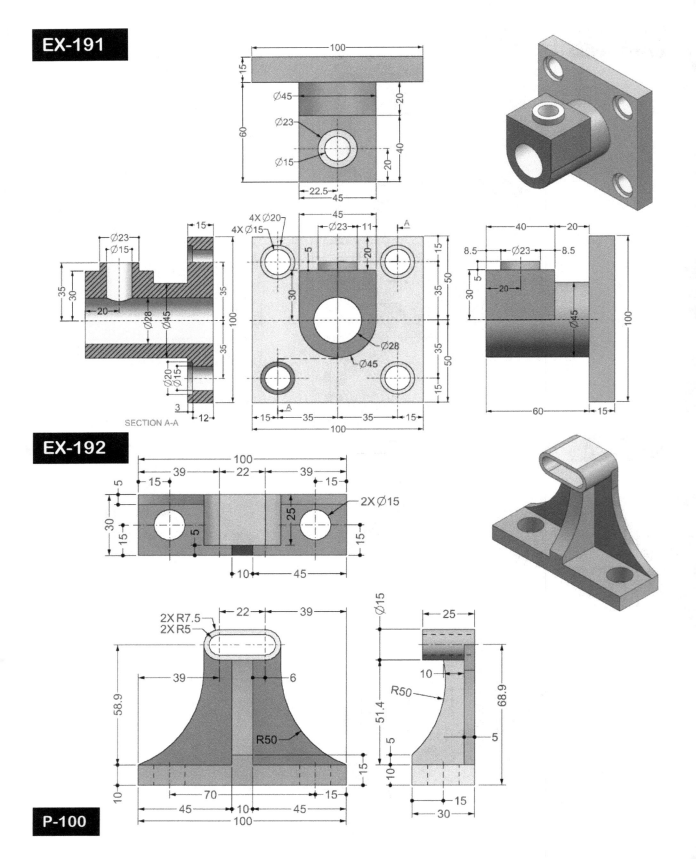

EX-191

EX-192

P-100

EX-193

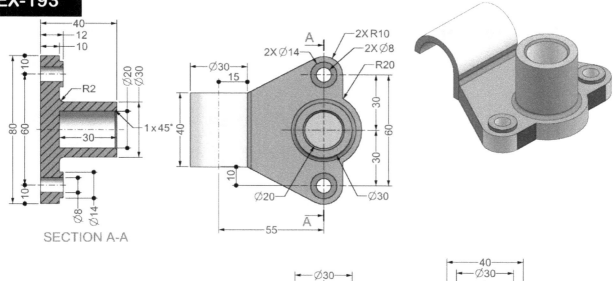

SECTION A-A

40
12
10
10
R2
80
60
Ø20
Ø30
1 x 45°
30
10
Ø8
Ø14

Ø30
15
2X Ø14
A
2X R10
2X Ø8
R20
40
30
60
30
10
Ø20
Ø30
55
A

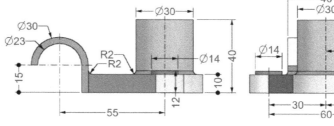

Ø30
Ø23
15
R2
R2
Ø30
Ø14
40
10
55
12

40
Ø30
Ø14
20
R3.2
40
10
12
30
30
60

EX-194

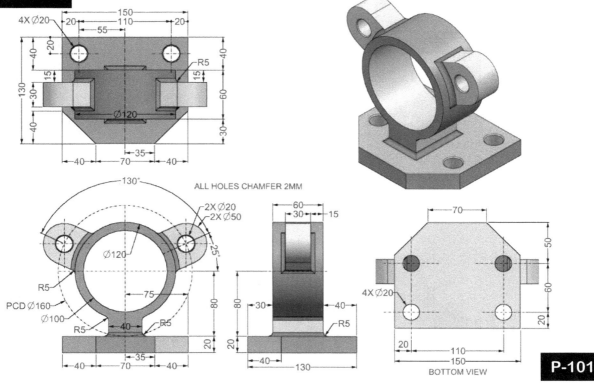

4X Ø20
150
20
110
20
55
20
40
40
15
R5
15
130
30
60
Ø120
40
30
40
70
40
35

ALL HOLES CHAMFER 2MM

130°
2X Ø20
2X Ø50
25°
Ø120
Ø100
75
80
R5
PCD Ø160
R5
40
R5
40
70
40
35
20

60
30
15
80
30
40
20
R5
40
130

70
50
60
4X Ø20
20
20
110
150

BOTTOM VIEW

P-101

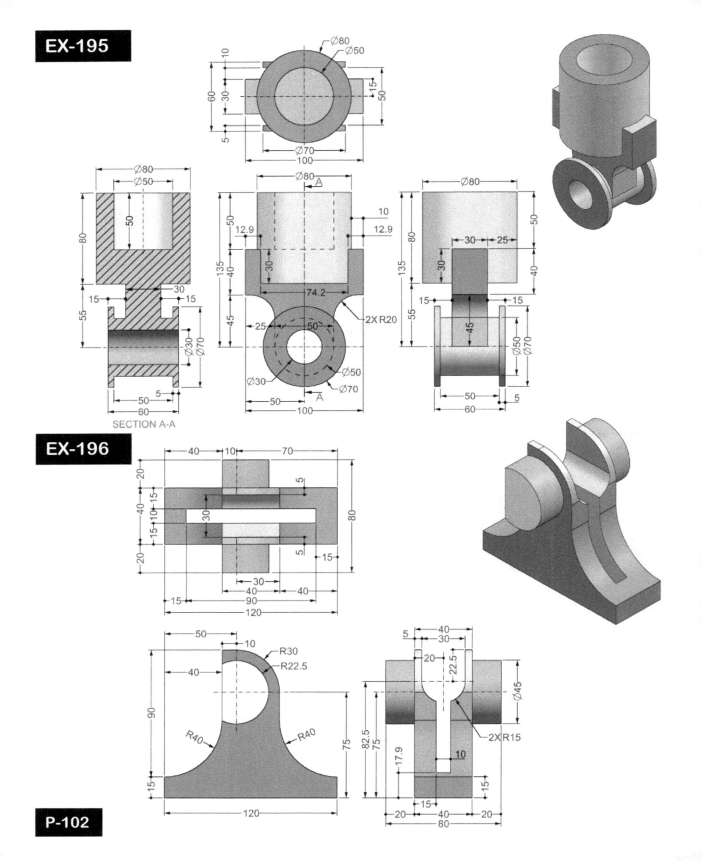

EX-195

Ø80
Ø50
10
60
30
15
50
5
Ø70
100

Ø80
Ø50
80
50
55
30
15
15
Ø30
Ø70
50
5
60
SECTION A-A

Ø80
A
50
40
135
45
10
12.9
12.9
30
74.2
2X R20
25
50
50
Ø30
Ø50
Ø70
100
A

Ø80
80
50
135
40
30
25
30
55
15
15
45
Ø50
Ø70
50
5
60

EX-196

40
10
70
20
20
40
15
10
15
15
5
30
80
5
15
30
40
40
15
90
120

50
10
R30
R22.5
40
90
R40
R40
75
15
120

40
5
30
20
22.5
Ø45
82.5
75
2X R15
17.9
10
15
15
20
40
20
80

P-102

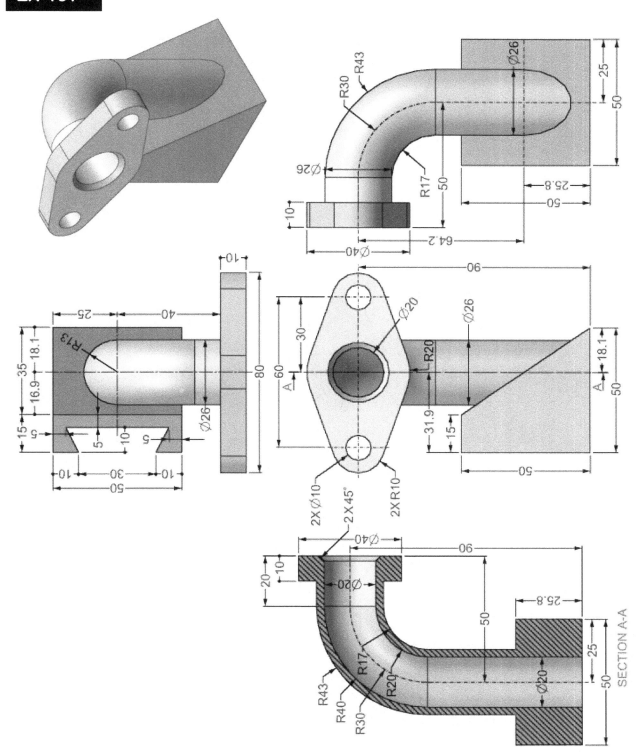

EX-197

2X Ø10
2 X 45°
2X R10

Ø20
R20
Ø26

R30
R43
Ø26
R17
Ø26
Ø40

R13
Ø26

SECTION A-A

P-103

6X Ø15 THRU ON PCD 90

Ø120

Ø50

Ø40

PCD Ø90

A

A

Ø120

Ø50

Ø40

15

10

Ø15

120

60°

60°

80

30

Ø10

SECTION A-A

B-B

5

10

Ø20

Ø30

PCD 54

VIEW B-B

Ø20

8X Ø10 THRU ON PCD 54

Ø30

Ø70

PCD Ø54

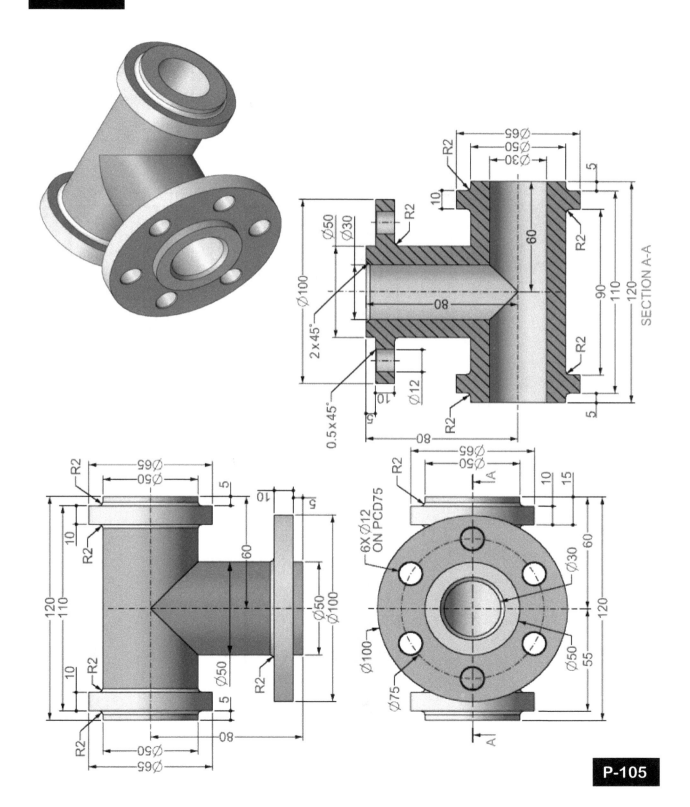

SECTION A-A

6X∅12
ON PCD75

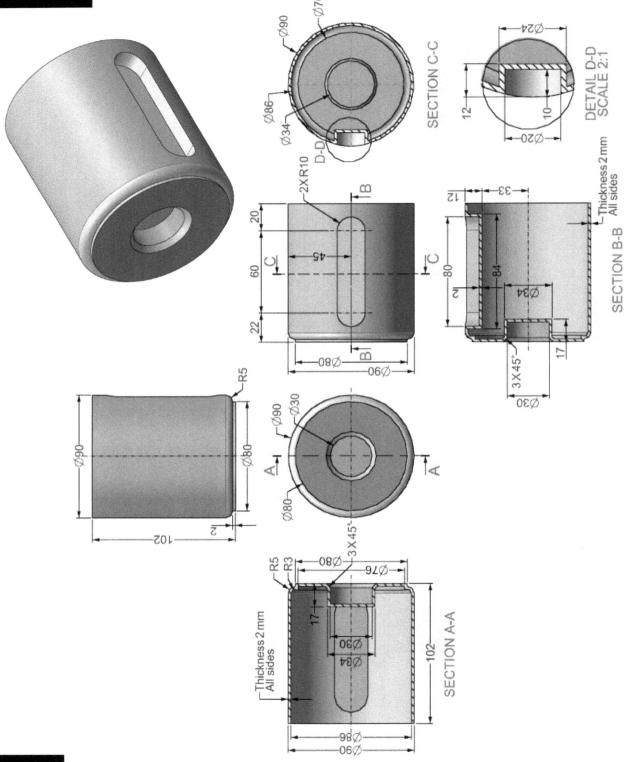

Ø76
Ø90
Ø86
Ø34
D-D

SECTION C-C

Ø24
12
10
Ø20

DETAIL D-D
SCALE 2:1

2XR10
B
20
C
45
60
22
Ø80
B
Ø90

Thickness 2 mm
All sides
12
33
80
84
2
Ø34
3 X 45°
17
Ø30

SECTION B-B

R5
Ø90
Ø80
2
102

Ø90
Ø30
A
A
Ø80

R5
R3
Ø80
3 X 45°
Ø76
17
Ø30
Ø84
102
Thickness 2 mm
All sides
Ø86
Ø90

SECTION A-A

Other useful books by CADIN360

1. 150 CAD Exercises

2. AutoCAD Exercises

3. CAD Exercises

4. 50+ SolidWorks Exercises

5. SolidWorks 200 Exercises

6. Autodesk Inventor Exercises

7. Catia Exercises

8. Siemens NX Exercises

www.ingramcontent.com/pod-product-compliance
Lightning Source LLC
Chambersburg PA
CBHW060447060326
40689CB00020B/4463